THAT I MAY KNOW HIM

BIBLE
MODULAR
SERIES

bju **press**®

Greenville, South Carolina

That I May Know Him

H. Douglas Garland, M.A.

Editor: Catherine Anderson
Designer: John Bjerk
Composition: Jennifer Hearing and Rebecca G. Zollinger

Photograph credits appear on page 132.

© 2002, 2010 BJU Press
Greenville, South Carolina 29609

ISBN 978-1-60682-055-1

15 14 13 12 11 10 9 8 7 6 5

CONTENTS

*I*ntroduction

A re you satisfied with the person you see in the mirror every morning?

Not your hair or your skin, but the person. You. Do you want to change you?

And not all change is good, so how do you point your change in the right direction?

It starts with God changing you the way only God can—from the inside. That's what salvation is. The Bible calls it regeneration or being born from above. You already are a changed person if you've truly been converted.

But good change, even though it ultimately comes from God, also involves your own choices. You've got to choose to obey what God says in His Word about how to change.

And this is what God says—in this case through Paul, someone who had changed a lot from what he used to be: "But we all, with open face beholding as in a glass the glory of the Lord, are changed into the same image from glory to glory, even as by the Spirit of the Lord" (2 Cor. 3:18).

In other words, start watching God through His Word. Pay attention to His glory, the innumerable things that make Him stand out. If you do that, you'll start to be changed into the same image, going from glory to glory to higher glory. God's Spirit can do this in you.

Where is God's glory most obvious? Where does it shine brightest? In His Son. "In him dwelleth all the fulness of the Godhead bodily," Paul says (Col. 2:9). Jesus Christ is "the brightness of (God's) glory, and the express image of his person" (Heb. 1:3).

So watch Jesus, and you'll change. Don't expect to understand everything He did and said. He lived on a higher plane while at the same time living on ours. He even said some things purposefully to confuse people—as a way of judging them for their unwillingness to understand (Matt. 13:13).

But that's not His heart toward God's children. To them He'd say, "Come unto me, all ye that labour and are heavy laden, and I will give you rest. Take my yoke upon you, and learn of me" (Matt. 11:28-29).

So come, learn, change.

The Beginning of the Gospel

In just two minutes, the bell would ring, signaling the start of the final driver's education class for the year. The state licensing agency opened at 9 A.M. the next day, and Frank Carlson dreamed of being the very first one in line. That is, if Mr. Johnson, the hardest teacher in school, gave him a passing grade. It all depended on the score of the final project, a paper on driver safety. That topic was obviously very important to Mr. Johnson. Each class had started with a short lecture on safety. Each class had ended with an exhortation to be responsible drivers.

Frank shuddered as the bell sounded and a nervous stillness descended over the room. Everyone saw the graded projects in the teacher's hand.

"Class, most of you will soon join the ranks of automobile drivers in our state. The projects were very fine and it will be a great pleasure for me to give many passing grades."

As Mr. Johnson handed back each graded project, he asked the student receiving the paper to state one rule of driver safety. The student glanced at the grade on his paper and then stated a principle. The instructor then reviewed that particular principle before handing back the next paper. The tension in the class rose as students took more of the basic rules. The last person might not have any rules left. Frank's face turned red as the teacher came toward his desk with only one paper in his hand. Kelly Brown had just used his idea and his mind was blank! The grade was a B+!

Frank said nervously, "Mr. Johnson, my father tells me that my actions speak louder than my words and . . . "

The class broke into hushed laughter as Mr. Johnson stopped Frank midsentence and gave him a thumbs up.

"We studied many rules, laws, and driving tips this semester. Now, the best thing you can do is follow Frank's advice. Your grade means almost nothing. Your actions on the road will speak to everyone about your training and your ability. People will not care about your A or B in this class with me. They will want to see a safe and courteous driver."

My parents told me many times that my actions would speak louder than my words. I got tired of hearing it. As the years pass, I more fully understand their admonitions to me. Talk is free. Action shows character and conviction. I want my friends to be people who back up their words with vigorous action. Tell me, yes; but show me too!

We will study together a man of great deeds as described by another man who valued action more than dialogue. Jesus Christ was the greatest teacher in the world. His eloquent simplicity communicated God's truth both to the scholar and to the child. Some people fail to see that His actions spoke just as mightily as His words. He spoke the truth. He lived the truth.

Most of us know people in church or in school that talk like Christians but don't live like Christians. We know from the Bible that a Christian's walk should match his talk.

The chasm between people's knowledge of what is right and their actions can be wide. Perhaps we see the same chasm in ourselves. It can be very uncomfortable. May I suggest that the problem may be a lack of real understanding about Jesus Christ? The apostle Paul shows us the bridge over this chasm when he declares the desire of his heart, "That I may know him" (Phil. 3:10). We will seek to see and to understand Jesus Christ through this study. Only then will our speech and our actions truly please God.

John Mark

Before looking at the Lord Jesus Christ, we need to spend some time examining how the message of Christ is transmitted to us today. If you and I cannot speak face to face, we are very comfortable talking to one another on the telephone or perhaps through e-mail. Obviously, our modern conveniences were not available two thousand years ago.

God simply used the life and writings of John Mark, an ordinary man, to communicate to us the great message of eternal life in Christ. Mark wrote his Gospel for the benefit of the ancient Roman people.

These people revolted against the Greeks' love of philosophy and talk. They wanted action. Mark simply told them about the deeds of Jesus. He also helped them to understand His words. A main purpose of this course is to give you the skills needed to see and to apply the deeds and words of Christ.

HISTORICAL LIGHT

Roman Facts

Historians regard the Roman civilization as one of the world's greatest. Consider the following facts:

Time: Centralized Roman power extended from 509 B.C. to A.D. 410. The Roman government in the East lasted until about A.D. 1400. Most modern governments are still infants compared to Rome!

Conquest: Rome conquered significant portions of the known world including parts of Europe, Africa, and Asia. Great armies would defeat a nation and then stay indefinitely to govern for Rome.

Language: The official language of the Roman Empire was Latin. In fact, the Gospel of Mark contains more Latin words than any other New Testament book. Spanish, Italian, and French are direct descendants of Latin. Many of our legal and scientific terms come from Latin words.

Architecture: The Romans built massive structures, many of which still exist today. Tourists often view the Roman Coliseum that was used for fights between gladiators and could even be flooded for naval battles. You can also still see Roman aqueducts that carried water over valleys to large cities.

Law: In 451 B.C. the Romans wrote down the basic precepts of law for society. The law allowed a landowner to cut down part of a tree that hung over his property. A person stealing another man's crops could be put to death. Justinian edited laws from the history of Rome and created what we know today as the Justinian Code. This document is the model for most legal systems of continental Europe.

Let's examine some of the facts of Mark's life. His full name, John Mark, reflected the cultural and ethnic diversity of the Roman world. *John* comes from a Hebrew word meaning "Jehovah has graciously given." *Mark,* on the other hand, was a very common Latin name.

Acts 12:12 indicates that Mark's mother lived in Jerusalem in a house large enough for a meeting of the apostles and the believers. They possibly used her house as a church. Living in Jerusalem may have given Mark the opportunity to see and to hear Jesus for himself. Many Bible scholars believe that Mark mentioned himself in his Gospel.

Mark, *by Guido Reni, Bob Jones University Collection*

> And they all forsook him, and fled. And there followed him a certain young man, having a linen cloth cast about his naked body; and the young men laid hold on him: And he left the linen cloth, and fled from them naked (Mark 14:50-52).

None of the other Gospels mention this seemingly minor incident. Confusion and betrayal surrounded Christ at His arrest.

Using Strong's Concordance

TEXT TOOLS

A concordance is a book that lists the chapter and verse locations of particular words used in the Bible. Some reference Bibles may also contain a short concordance. By looking up the words *Mark* and *Marcus*, we can find many references to the author of the second Gospel. Many students and scholars believe that the concordance is the most useful of all the Bible study tools. You will have many opportunities to use one in this course.

Could it be that Mark turns his focus from Christ to himself for just a moment to tell us that he was present at this terrible event?

We may assume that Mark saw many of the events in the early chapters of Acts since he lived in Jerusalem and had a close relationship with the apostles. Peter calls Mark "my son" which indicates that Peter had led the young man to saving faith in Christ (I Pet. 5:13). Since Mark's father is not mentioned, we may assume that he was dead at this time. Barnabas and Saul took Mark to the vibrant church in Antioch (Acts 12:25). When the Lord called these two men to preach the gospel in the regions beyond, they took

---

HISTORICAL LIGHT

The Greek Alphabet

Latin was the language of law and politics, but Greek was the common language of the people. Mark wrote in Koine Greek so that the average person anywhere in the Roman world could learn about Jesus. You are very familiar with some different forms of English letters—capital and lower case. In Greek, an uncial was the form of a letter used when writing quickly was important. Most business contracts and personal correspondence used uncials. How many Greek letters do you recognize in the picture of Mark's Gospel on the next page?

name	capital	lower	uncial	name	capital	lower	uncial
Alpha	A	α	λ	Nu	N	ν	N
Beta	B	β	Ḅ	Xi	Ξ	ξ	Ʒ
Gamma	Γ	γ	Γ	Omicron	O	o	O
Delta	Δ	δ	Δ	Pi	Π	π	Π
Epsilon	E	ε	Є	Rho	P	ρ	Ρ
Zeta	Z	ζ	Z	Sigma	Σ	σ	C
Eta	H	η	H	Tau	T	τ	T
Theta	Θ	θ	Θ	Upsilon	Y	υ	Υ
Iota	I	ι	Ɩ	Phi	Φ	φ	Φ
Kappa	K	κ	K	Chi	X	χ	X
Lambda	Λ	λ	λ	Psi	Ψ	ψ	†
Mu	M	μ	M	Omega	Ω	ω	ⱳ

Mark as a helper (Acts 13:5). After the incident with Elymas the sorcerer, Mark returned to his home in Jerusalem perhaps due to his youth or out of fear (Acts 13:13). Conceivably, he came back under the influence of Peter's ministry in Jerusalem. Later, Barnabas and Paul went their separate ways because Barnabas wanted to take Mark on their next trip and Paul did not (Acts 15:37-39).

Peter and Paul both mention in their letters that Mark was present with them in various locations. Paul's references to Mark (Col. 4:10; Philem. 24; II Tim. 4:11) indicate that he traveled with the apostle and that he performed valuable services in the ministry.

We may conclude that Paul's estimate of Mark's character had improved over time. Peter tells us that Mark was with him in "Babylon" (I Pet. 5:13). Scholars debate whether this was the actual city named Babylon or a figure of speech for Rome. In either case, the implication is that Mark was well known to the churches and that he was working with Peter.

Mark's association with the apostles allowed him to hear great preaching about Christ, to see the power of God in lives, and to watch as these men wrote instructional letters to the churches. We would not classify Mark as one of the great men of the Bible like Peter or Paul. However, God put Mark in a very strategic location to observe and to digest more of Christianity's development than perhaps any other person. God was simply preparing Mark to write the story of Jesus Christ for our benefit!

Early References to Mark's Gospel

A quick reading of the Gospel of Mark reveals that many of the events occurred outside Jerusalem. How is it that Mark could write about Christ's experiences prior to His arrival in Jerusalem where Mark lived?

We know from the verses above that Mark spent much time with Peter who was with Jesus during most of His public ministry. Peter undoubtedly told the story of Christ time and time again as he traveled and as people came to him. It makes sense then that Mark may have recorded the preaching of Peter about the life of Christ.

God raised up a group of men that we know as the "church fathers" following the times of the apostles. We have various

HISTORICAL LIGHT

The Canon of Scripture

Canon reminds us of a great military weapon used to shoot explosives at the enemy! In biblical studies, the word refers to a standard of measurement, like a yardstick or a ruler. During the time of the apostles and in the years following, many books and letters circulated among believers. Some of these writings were obviously defective or of inferior quality. The Christians agreed that the following "measurements" showed which writings were authoritative and should be included in the New Testament.

1. The book must be written by an apostle or someone closely associated with an apostle.
2. The book must agree with the teaching of the rest of Scripture.
3. The book must be universally accepted by diverse parts of the church.
4. The book must show evidences of being inspired by the Holy Spirit.

God used the early Christians to compile the proper writings into the New Testament. Over the centuries, God used men to copy the books and to translate them into the languages of the world. We may have absolute confidence that our English Bible is God's Word to us.

writings from these men about the apostles and about early church history. These leaders tell us that Mark's Gospel contains the teachings of Peter. Eusebius quotes Papias (about A.D. 125 in Asia Minor) as saying,

> Mark, having become the interpreter of Peter, wrote accurately what he remembered of the things said or done by Christ, but not in order. For he took thought for one thing not to omit any of the things he had heard nor to falsify anything in them.

Eusebius also quotes Irenaeus from about A.D. 175 in Gaul:

> But after the departure of these (Peter and Paul), Mark, the disciple and interpreter of Peter, even he has delivered to us in writing the things which were preached by Peter.

Scholars love to examine even the smallest details of biblical history. The majority, both ancient and modern, confirm that Mark's Gospel is an accurate record of the teachings and actions of Christ. We can have absolute confidence in God's communication to us. Our job is to learn how to listen to it.

Who Is Jesus Christ?

Peter was a decisive man who generally got right to the point. Mark seems to follow his teacher's style by giving us a brief and yet powerful introduction to Jesus: "The beginning of the gospel of Jesus Christ, the Son of God" (Mark 1:1).

Mark's view of the person and work of Christ is the central focus of the entire book. Our understanding of Jesus' actions and teachings depends upon our ability to see the truths expressed in the very first verse of the book.

First, let's examine the person of Christ through His names and titles. Keep in mind that names in the ancient world carried much more meaning than names do today. *Jesus* is the Greek form of the common Jewish name meaning "Jehovah saves." It is equivalent to the Hebrew name *Joshua*. God first promised a deliverer from sin in Genesis 3:15 and then repeated the promise in various ways and at different times. The story of the Old Testament revolves around the hopes and preparations for the one who would deliver God's people from their sins.

Near the time of Jesus' birth, the angel of the Lord spoke to Joseph saying,

> Joseph, thou son of David, fear not to take unto thee Mary thy wife: for that which is conceived in her is of the Holy Ghost. And she shall bring forth a son, and thou shalt call his name Jesus: for he shall save his people from their sins (Matt. 1:20, 21).

The name *Jesus* identifies the subject of Mark's Gospel with God's intention to save His people. It also shows us that Jesus was fully human. He had a human body that required food and rest. Jesus often called Himself the "Son of man" which reinforced His humanity to the hearers. He was born just like any other man except that He was conceived by the Holy Spirit. As a man, Jesus understood the frailties of humanity and exercised great compassion on those in need. Since the Holy Spirit conceived Jesus in Mary's womb, Jesus did not possess a sin nature. He did not sin against God as you and I are so prone to do. In every respect, Jesus was the perfect man.

The word *christ* is not a name, but is rather a title for the Jewish messiah. Both the Greek term *christ* and the Hebrew term *messiah* mean "anointed one." The Old Testament records the practice of pouring oil on the heads of men specifically set apart for three types of divine service.

Samuel anointed Saul and David as kings of Israel (I Sam. 9:16; 16:13). Moses anointed Aaron as the high priest (Exod. 29:7). Elijah anointed Elisha as a prophet (I Kings 19:16). The Israelites clearly looked for an anointed leader that would deliver them from bondage.

> The Spirit of the Lord God is upon me; because the Lord hath **anointed** me to preach good tidings unto the meek; he hath sent me to bind up the brokenhearted, to proclaim liberty to the captives, and the opening of the prison to them that are bound; to proclaim the acceptable year of the Lord, and the day of vengeance of our God; to comfort all that mourn; to appoint unto them that mourn in Zion, to give unto them beauty for ashes, the oil of joy for mourning, the garment of praise for the spirit of heaviness; that they might be called trees of righteousness, the planting of the Lord, that he might be glorified (Isa. 61:1-3).

Jesus performed the duties of a prophet by teaching God's truth to all men. He acted as a priest by sacrificing Himself to reconcile sinners to God. Believers follow Him as their king. One day, Jesus will be King over all mankind. Jesus was the fulfillment of the Jewish expectation for a messiah. John the Baptist announced His coming to the nation (John 1:29-37). A few of Jesus' disciples quickly recognized Him as the Messiah (John 1:43-51). Others took much longer. Only after the Resurrection did most of the disciples truly understand Jesus' position. Many of the Jewish leaders rejected Him altogether. Mark tells us plainly who Jesus is from the very beginning of his book. We can then watch and learn from Jesus as He reveals Himself to mankind.

What Is Sin?

Choose the best answer.

A. Sin is simply a mistake—writing the number 5 on a math test instead of 3.

B. Sin is an accident—tripping over a baseball bat in your yard.

C. Sin is a missed opportunity—not being able to go to the mountains on the weekend.

D. Sin is the poor appearance of an object—my brother's wrecked car.

E. Sin is breaking the law of God—stealing or lying.

People often use the word *sin* in a casual manner to refer to something accidental or unfortunate. According to the Bible, sin is a very serious issue. What are the implications of man's sin according to the following verses?

Whosoever committeth sin transgresseth also the law: for sin is the transgression of the law (I John 3:4).

For all have sinned, and come short of the glory of God (Rom. 3:23).

For the wages of sin is death; but the gift of God is eternal life through Jesus Christ our Lord (Rom. 6:23).

Mark also tells us that Jesus was the "Son of God." Jewish leaders of the day well understood that the Messiah would be God's Son, and therefore He would be equal to God (Matt. 26:63).

The grammar of the original language indicates that Mark is focusing on Jesus' character or quality as deity. While studying Mark's Gospel together, we will see that only God could do many of the things that Jesus did. His Resurrection from the dead and His ascension into heaven forever sealed this truth in the disciples' minds.

Why Did Jesus Come?

Mark begins his story with an exalted and honoring proclamation about the identity of Jesus. If we understand who He is, then logically we need to investigate why He came to earth and what He did while here. Jesus Himself reveals the answers to us:

> And he said unto them, Let us go into the next towns, that I may preach there also: for therefore came I forth (Mark 1:38).

> When Jesus heard it, he saith unto them, They that are whole have no need of the physician, but they that are sick: I came not to call the righteous, but sinners to repentance (Mark 2:17).

> For even the Son of man came not to be ministered unto, but to minister, and to give his life a ransom for many (Mark 10:45).

Mankind honors great political leaders, sports stars, and military heroes by meeting their every need and whim. Higher rank or accomplishment brings ever-increasing money, fame, and respect.

Those attaining high achievement expect "royal" treatment. Jesus Christ, the greatest man ever, walked a different path. Notice in the verses above that Jesus' ministry focused on the common people in the villages, on the sick, and on sinners. He came to teach, to heal, and to meet the needs of hurting men. His greatest act was His death in place of sinners. God justly sentenced man to death for breaking the law and for turning from righteousness. Jesus interceded by dying in man's place so that man could be free from sin. In fact, the word *give* implies that Jesus was in full control of His situation and did not lose His life as a criminal or by accident. He purposed to die for man. Mark will show us the purposes and heart of Christ in every chapter.

Remember that Mark starts his Gospel with "the beginning of the gospel of Jesus Christ." The word *gospel* means "good news." A beginning implies a continuation. Mark wrote possibly thirty years after the time of Christ. The proclamation of sins forgiven was still good news to all. It should be the same for us today.

Our Task

Let's briefly review some facts that Mark presents to us. Jesus Christ is fully human and fully divine. As a man, He can sympathize with our weaknesses and our failures. As God, He is able to show us the truth and to relieve our problems. We cannot understand how Jesus could be both God and man, but it is the clear teaching of the Bible. The great prophet Isaiah proclaimed, "Therefore the Lord himself shall give you a sign; Behold, a virgin shall conceive, and bear a son, and shall call his name Immanuel" (Isa. 7:14). The Gospel of Matthew tells us that *Emmanuel* means, "God with us" (Matt. 1:23). Jesus is the bridge between God and man, and also between our failures and the wonderful life that God wants us to have.

As we study the Gospel of Mark, let's be alert to Jesus' humanity. Let's look for His words and actions as God. Christ continually interacted with various people. Some are much like you and me. Jesus completely transformed those that chose to believe and to follow Him. Mark started off as a weak young man who deserted his friends. He ended up as a choice instrument in the hand of God. Peter began as an impetuous fisherman. Jesus molded him into a servant who literally changed the entire world. We can know the same Jesus and experience the same change as Peter and Mark.

Review Questions

1. Who called Mark "my son"?

2. What city did Mark live in?

3. Who refused to take Mark on a mission trip?

4. What does the name "Jesus" mean?

5. Whose teaching about Jesus did Mark record?

6. What is the Greek word that means "messiah"?

7. Who announced Jesus' coming to the Jewish nation?

8. What type of book lists chapter and verse locations for words used in the Bible?

9. What does the term *gospel* mean?

10. To whom did Mark write his Gospel?

11. Why did Mark have two names?

12. How could Mark write about Jesus when he did not have first-hand knowledge about all of Jesus' life?

13. According to the verses in this chapter, what was the function of the Holy Spirit in Jesus' life?

14. Why did Jesus come to earth?

15. How did Mark imitate his teachers?

Christ and the Multitudes

2

"Load up! Let's move out!" rang through the house. Dad signaled the start of another car trip. Jared and Tessa moved with more speed than usual as they gathered up the last of the supplies and food. This time, the family was going on vacation for ten days to a cabin in a national park.

Dad looked forward to the trout fishing. Mom simply wanted to rest and maybe work on a cross-stitch project. Jared and Tessa had other plans.

"Dad, I have a question." Jared spoke tentatively about two hours into the trip.

"Let me guess, you need to stop at a rest area," Mom responded while Dad changed lanes on the highway.

Jared and Tessa shook their heads.

Dad turned down the CD player and cast a puzzled glance through the rearview mirror at Jared.

Jared started, "You know that Tessa and I get bored at the cabin after a couple of days. We thought about hiking to that little village to the east of the park for a day. It's only three miles and we could be back by supper."

Mom and Dad looked at each other cautiously.

Tessa spoke up this time, "We want to watch the man who makes the chocolate candies for our school fundraisers. He told us to visit his shop the next time we came to the cabin. Besides, as soon as school starts in the fall, the teachers assign a report on life in small towns. I need all the information that I can get."

Dad responded in an unusual way, "Did the two of you realize that small towns attracted Jesus too?"

This time, Jared and Tessa looked at each other.

"I will approve the trip with two conditions," Dad continued. "You must find out what Jesus did in the villages of His day and then imitate Him in at least one way."

"What's the other condition?" Tessa asked.

"Be back before supper!"

Jared and Tessa kept busy learning about Jesus in the Gospels and then had a great day in the village. They decided to imitate Jesus by giving out the small New Testaments that Dad kept in the van. The vacation was fantastic!

The Master Teacher

Jared and Tessa's father was correct in his statement that Jesus spent much time in the villages and small towns of Israel. Mark shows us that Jesus constantly traveled from one place to the next.

> And he said unto them, Let us go into the next towns, that I may preach there also: for therefore came I forth. And he preached in their synagogues throughout all Galilee, and cast out devils (Mark 1:38, 39).

Great multitudes often gathered to see and hear Jesus. Sometimes the crowd was so huge that Jesus could not even eat! Mark 12:37 tells us that "the common people heard him gladly." What attracted Jesus to the small cities and villages? What attracted the multitudes of Israel to Him? Much of this book will seek to answer those questions.

Let's focus first of all on the fact that Jesus was a master teacher. We believe that He was the greatest teacher ever! Keep in mind that Jesus is God's Son, and therefore He is God. This gives Jesus a perspective on truth and reality that sinful humans do not have. He could explain God's view on every issue of life. Jesus is also a man and as a man, He understands the rigors and challenges of living for God on earth. Putting His two natures together means that He could teach God's truth in human terms so everyone could understand.

Teaching is hard work. Ask any of your instructors! Often after teaching the multitude, Jesus would have a private session for the disciples. We will study some of those times in another chapter. Also, teachers in the ancient world normally stayed in one place and the students came to them. Jesus traveled from village to village so that everyone could hear the message from God. It's easy to understand why He needed rest.

I have traveled to many places both in this country and around the world. Talking to people, eating various types of food, listening to strange languages, and watching many activities leads me to a simple conclusion: people are basically the same. They have similar desires, hopes, and difficulties. The main problem throughout history is sin, which results in a broken relationship to God. Jesus knew the problem well. He taught the people of His day about knowing God personally. His teachings are as fresh today as they were two thousand years ago. Let's look at some of Jesus' words so that our relationship to God might flourish.

The Kingdom of God

Jesus started a new phase of His work when He entered Galilee (Mark 1:16) and started preaching a simple but profound message. Notice that Jesus is taking the message directly to the people. Both Mark and Jesus seem to assume that the reader and the hearer would understand the basics of the kingdom. Since we are removed both in time and in culture from their situation, we may need to consider some foundational principles before looking at Jesus' specific teaching.

A kingdom certainly implies a king. It also implies a people or land to rule, and a means by which that rule is carried out. Your younger brother may make a crown and dress up like royalty. He may then proclaim that he is king over the entire country. He has a land to rule but does not have the means to carry out his rule. You will probably consider his actions to be humorous. To the Romans, the concept of a kingdom was no laughing matter. They lived and worked under the authority of the Emperor who had almost absolute power. The Roman armies regularly crushed any threat, or any rumored threat, to their power. They had controlled Palestine for about ninety years when Jesus started preaching. The Romans would not be happy about the kingdom of God.

But for the Jews, the kingdom of God would be good news. They looked for a man to take the throne of David (Isa. 9:7) and then to reestablish the sovereignty of Israel. Their hatred of foreign governments blinded them to the fact that the kingdom of God starts as a personal relationship to Him and that the political phase would come later in time.

Let's examine Jesus' teaching about entering into the kingdom.

> Now after that John was put in prison, Jesus came into Galilee, preaching the gospel of the kingdom of God, And saying, The time is fulfilled, and the kingdom of God is at hand: repent ye, and believe the gospel (Mark 1:14, 15).

John the Baptist preached about the kingdom, and also that a much greater man was about to appear (Mark 1:7, 8). John's public ministry ended when he was imprisoned. It seems logical that the next major event would be the appearance of this great man.

Life in Galilee

Galilee was well known in the Roman world for fine agricultural products. Most families in the region farmed and raised livestock. Fishing was the main industry in the towns and villages bordering the Sea of Galilee. The region's natural resources supported the largest population in Palestine and perhaps one of the wealthiest.

Nazareth, Jesus' boyhood home, was typical of most villages of the day. A major trade route passed nearby and probably gave the village a steady stream of outside merchants and visitors. Most homes were made of stone or clay bricks. Houses were tightly packed together for mutual security. People dumped their garbage on the few narrow streets. The center of town contained a Jewish synagogue and was the location of the main religious and social event of the week. Ladies went to the local well at least once a day for the family's water. The open-air market contained local produce and household products. Each purchase required an intense price negotiation between buyer and seller. All boys learned a trade and some attended formal Jewish schools. Girls prepared for marriage by gaining the skills needed to manage a household.

Jesus' first announcement of the kingdom came in Galilee. Many of the Jews would recognize this as the realization of Isaiah 9:1, 2 where the prophet indicates that Galilee would see a great light. Jesus also teaches that the fulfillment of Old Testament promises about the Messiah was very near. The clear implication is that the person making the announcement, Jesus, was none other than the king. All the blessings and benefits of the kingdom would be found in and through Him.

Foreign Domination of Palestine

Roman history is divided into two great periods. The Roman Republic (509-27 B.C.) saw Rome's expansion throughout much of the known world. The great general Pompey conquered Jerusalem in 63 B.C. and brought Palestine under Roman domination. Decapolis, a league of ten Greek cities built to the east and south of Galilee by Roman officials, provided a base for control and often provoked the Jewish inhabitants. The Roman Empire (27 B.C.–A.D. 476) governed by a long series of emperors. Tiberius (A.D. 14-37), emperor during Christ's life, used a succession of procurators and vassal kings to control the provinces. Pontius Pilate ruled Judea for the emperor through taxation, military operations, and civil courts. He allowed the Jews to have some religious courts and limited civil power.

Herod Antipas ruled Galilee and Perea for Rome during the time of Christ's ministry. He built the city of Tiberias on top of an old cemetery near the western shore of the Sea of Galilee. Most Jews despised this city honoring the Roman emperor.

Baptism of John — **Year 1** — Mark 1:1-15

John Imprisoned

Parable of the Sower

Jairus's Daughter

Transfiguration — **Year 2** — Mark 1:16-5:43

Last Supper

Ascension — **Year 3** — Mark 6:1-16:20

If the kingdom of God were a political movement, you would expect Jesus to announce the formation of an army or a government. Instead, he turned the people's attention to the real problem. The word *repent* means "to change the mind" or "to change direction." Jesus preached that man has a sin problem. That sin must be acknowledged and forsaken. He also announced the necessity of faith, or belief in the good news. Abraham, the father of the nation, had believed God in very difficult circumstances. Now the Jews of Galilee must do the same. To enter the kingdom, they must believe in Jesus as their King and turn away from their sins.

The Gospel of Mark records about fourteen occasions when Jesus taught specifically about the kingdom. We will see in the following chapters that His actions confirm His claims as King. The multitudes and religious leaders eventually rejected Jesus and His teachings about the kingdom. They stubbornly held onto their traditions, culture, and religious heritage. Man has not changed much over the centuries. We still prefer to make our own rules for a relationship with God and for our behavior. In a political kingdom, a man is quickly imprisoned and punished for failing to obey the orders of the king. The same is true in spiritual matters. For our own good, we need to enter the kingdom according to God's design.

The Kingdom in Parables

Jesus was in the middle of another long, busy day. The scribes had accused Him of having a very wicked association with Satan (Mark 3:22-30). Then some of Jesus' family members had prompted a discussion about the priority of spiritual relationships (Mark 3:31-35). At the close of the day, Jesus took a boat trip to the other side of Galilee and fell asleep during the voyage. A great storm threatened the boat when Jesus simply uttered, "Peace, be still," to calm the sea (Mark 4:39).

Between these events, Jesus taught great multitudes as He sat in a boat and the people sat on the shore. Mark indicates that this was a prolonged session. Many regard this day as the very climax of Jesus' great ministry in Galilee. He used a story-like teaching method known as a parable to relate spiritual truths in ordinary

The Sea of Galilee

The Jewish Tradition of Parables

The word *parable* in Greek means "to place beside" and therefore "to compare." Using a ruler, we can determine the length of a candy bar. The candy bar does not change in any way, but we understand its size better when we compare it to the ruler. Jewish teachers often told stories about everyday events to explain truths that otherwise may have been unclear to the listener. Parables are common in Jewish writings and in the Old Testament. Look up the following parables and write the meaning using one sentence.

Judges 9:8-15 _____

II Samuel 12:1-4 _____

Isaiah 5:1-7 _____

_____

events. Some folks would dismiss a parable as just a nice story. To them, the deeper truths were concealed. Parables were intended to make people think about spiritual issues. The more serious listeners might be rewarded with fuller explanations in private or with additional capacity to understand (Mark 4:24, 25). Jesus generally tried to communicate one central truth in each parable. Many of the details exist only to tell the story. The details have minimal spiritual importance. He often ended a parable with, "If any man have ears to hear, let him hear" (Mark 4:23). Let's make sure that our ears are open as Jesus relates three parables about farming that teach us about the kingdom.

Parable of the Soils

Jesus told a story that we might know as the parable of the sower. Some also call it the parable of the soils. A farmer would use a wooden plow pulled by oxen to break up the hard dirt. At the right time, he would walk through the field and throw handfuls of seed onto the prepared ground. The seed grew and prospered depending upon where it landed. Jesus points out four types of soil. The seed was the same in each case. The results depended upon the soil.

The "way side" was actually a path or small road that ran through the field. Birds immediately ate those seeds, which yielded no result for the farmer. Jesus later told the disciples that this soil represented hearers who are indifferent to spiritual truth. We might describe these with the proverb "In one ear and out the other." Notice that these people do hear the Word. It simply has no effect. The stony ground represents an area with thin soil covering a hard limestone rock. Seed germinates quickly in the warm damp soil, but withers as the summer heat increases. Jesus said that these people are comfortable with spiritual matters as long as things are easy. But as soon as trouble starts, they renounce the truth and depart. The third soil is very good but has heavy dense thorns growing in it. The thorns choke the sprouting seed and again the farmer gets nothing. These hearers place more value on material possessions than on spiritual reality. Last, Jesus describes the good soil. It yields a huge harvest. Some within this group produce more than others do. These folks not only hear the Word of God, they respond to it. The farmer obviously delights in the rich harvest.

What was Jesus trying to teach in the parable of the soils? He explained each major part to the disciples in Mark 4:14-20. Notice that the farmer spread seed on every part of his field. God intends that every man hear His Word.

The result depends upon the soil. If we push the details of the story too far, we might conclude that a man is incapable of producing a harvest or a suitable response to the Word due to his surroundings. "I cannot be responsible for the rock under me," could be interpreted as "God made me with a love for things, therefore I cannot respond to His Word." Jesus told the story so that the serious hearers would recognize the dangers of casual religion, emotionalism, and materialism. They can then weed those things out of their lives and become productive for the Lord.

Notice also that Jesus tells two additional shorter stories as footnotes to the parable of the soils. Each of these reinforces the idea that change is possible. In Mark 4:21, 22 Jesus relates a common scene in the ancient world.

People lit small oil lamps at night and placed them on a candlestick to give light to the household. Jesus tells them that just as the lamp gives light to the darkness, so God wants to reveal the hidden things of His Word to all who will receive it. He does not want to conceal the good news of salvation. He simply states it so that those who are dull of hearing have a better opportunity to understand it over time. The key is to respond properly. Notice in the next story that those who hear and respond properly are given more truth (Mark 4:24, 25). Change is possible as we listen and apply the Word to our lives. The parables hid truth to those who refused it and exposed truth to those who wanted it.

Parable of the Growing Seed

Jesus' next parable related truth that was both familiar and perplexing to the farmer. He simply stated in the story that God's kingdom grows like a seed planted in the ground. The plant passes through normal stages of development. It sprouts, grows the blade, then the ear, and afterwards the grain. The farmer can then harvest the grain for his benefit. As the farmer inspects his fields day by day, he cannot understand how the seed develops and produces the harvest. It simply grows under the direction of God's power in nature.

Mature Christians often look back over their lives with amazement at how God directed them through various stages of growth. The power and energy pushing them toward the harvest was not of human origin. Jesus told Nicodemus that the Holy Spirit, like the wind, germinated the seeds of salvation in man's heart (John 3). John the Baptist proclaimed that Jesus would baptize believers with the Holy Spirit (Mark 1:8). It seems that God uses His Spirit to develop the lives of believers into a bountiful harvest. Jesus' point is that the growth is impossible to understand fully, but that it does lead to positive results. Bible scholars debate whether this growth refers to the kingdom as a whole or to individual believers. Since the kingdom is made up of individuals, it seems to apply to both. We can rejoice that God works in our lives and has a definite design for us.

Small Seeds for a Large Nation

J. Hudson Taylor (1832-1905) dedicated his entire adult life to reaching the millions of China. Over the years, the Lord used Hudson Taylor to raise huge sums of money for the work in China, to establish twenty mission stations with over eight hundred missionaries, and to lead thousands to Christ. His legacy of answered prayer and ceaseless work still inspires missionaries today. Equally important, Taylor was the driving force behind evangelizing a massive, pagan nation for Christ.

Two seemingly small events mark the beginning of Taylor's spiritual life. As a teenager, he had drifted away from his parents' Christian faith and values. On a day off from his work in a bank, he was bored and picked up a small gospel tract from his father's library. The title, "It is Finished," gripped his heart as he understood for the first time Christ's power to save. Little did he know at the time that his mother, who was seventy miles away, was intensely praying for his salvation that very hour. The effects of a single gospel tract and a mother's prayer eventually shook the nation of China.

What could God do through you?

Parable of the Mustard Seed

The final parable recorded by Mark is similar to the second one. Jesus often repeated His teachings so that the disciples and others might better understand. Keep in mind that the Jews of the day looked for a strong political kingdom that would drive out foreign rulers and reestablish the nation of Israel. They wanted immediate action. Mark relates the story of the mustard plant.

The tiny seeds are placed in the ground and over time the plant grows mightily. Man uses the plant for food, and the birds

31

use it for shelter. God's kingdom would start out small and hardly noticeable. At maturity, the kingdom will be great and beneficial to all. Jesus' hearers marveled at the eventual size of the mustard plant compared to its humble beginnings. In time, they would likewise understand that Jesus' ministry was simply the small and obscure beginning of the kingdom. The growth would be enormous. We can be confident that the kingdom of God will continue to grow and to prosper.

The Kingdom for Common People

Jesus began His ministry by preaching very plainly about the kingdom of God. The Jewish religious leaders rejected Jesus' message just as they had rejected John the Baptist's. But at least for a while, the great multitudes of Galilee flocked to hear the greatest teacher ever. Jesus perceived that many did not understand and so He began to use parables to further encourage understanding and belief. One day, Jesus traveled to Nazareth, His hometown, and taught in the synagogue (Mark 6:1-6). Many family members attended the service. They could not comprehend how Jesus could teach so well and heal so many. Their failure to understand His teaching and His identity as the Christ led them to foolishly reject Him to their own peril.

And he could there do no mighty work, save that he laid his hands upon a few sick folk, and healed them. And he marvelled because of their unbelief. And he went round about the villages, teaching (Mark 6:5, 6).

Mark indicates that the people's lack of faith limited what Jesus could do for them. Their needs remained because they responded improperly to the King. It seems too that Jesus expected better from them. They knew Him from childhood. They had plainly heard the Word of God. The miracles and healings attested to the truth of His preaching. When Jesus could do no more for them, He simply departed to tell others who perhaps would respond according to God's plan.

The majority of us are like the multitudes of Jesus' day. We hear the Word of God, and yet many times we don't understand it. A decision then confronts us. When we earnestly try to understand and to believe, we make the right choice, which yields great benefit. On the other hand, we can choose to ignore the Word. The consequences can be devastating. Jared and Tessa were puzzled at first by their father's request to find out what Jesus did in the villages. Their proper response led to a great privilege – that of sharing the gospel – and their vacation went from boring to fantastic! Jesus can fantastically transform us provided that we respond to the simple teaching of His Word.

Review Questions

1. Jesus was both man and what?

2. What is man's main problem?

3. In what region did Jesus begin His preaching ministry?

4. Who anticipated a king to occupy David's throne?

5. Who prophesied that Galilee would see a great light?

6. What two things do parables do with the truth?

7. What represent worldly possessions in the parable of the soils?

8. What do people who respond properly to God's Word receive more of?

9. Jesus compared the kingdom to what kind of seed?

10. What was Jesus' boyhood hometown?

11. Why was Jesus a good teacher?

12. Why did John the Baptist and Jesus preach the common theme of repentance?

13. Why did the Jews dislike the Romans?

14. How do people enter God's kingdom?

15. What is casual religion?

Christ and the Sick

3

John Sizemore and his group of friends piled onto the bus with about twenty other juniors and seniors. The bus headed toward the Nelson home, which was about five miles into the country from the church. Everyone looked forward to the monthly Sunday evening singspirations and especially to the food. Several cars were already in the driveway as the bus pulled up. Some of the guys immediately started the usual basketball game while the girls gathered around the patio to talk. In about thirty minutes the pizza arrived and Mr. Nelson called the teens into the house. Once inside, John noticed three or four people that he did not know. After prayer, the guys waited impatiently for the girls to get their pizza, chips, and drink. The Nelsons then quickly moved out of the way as fourteen hungry young men reduced five large pepperoni pizzas to empty cardboard boxes.

"Do you guys always eat like this?" asked one of the girls that John did not know.

After wiping the pizza sauce off his fingers, John extended his hand and formally introduced himself to Megan Matthews. She was visiting her uncle for a couple of weeks and really seemed to enjoy the large group of teens.

After the food, the youth pastor led the teens in several hymns and choruses. He then asked if anyone had a prayer request or a testimony that he wanted to share. Megan shyly raised her hand and began to speak, "This has been a great evening for me! My church in Grand Junction is very small. We have maybe five teens, so we don't often do much together. Praise the Lord that we can sing and have a great time together. You might remember to pray for my mom. She has a disease that is very painful. I can hardly pronounce its name. God has been very good to us in every way."

John "worked things out" so that he sat near Megan on the bus ride back to the church. He asked her how she could be so calm and peaceful while talking about her mother.

Megan responded, "It's not always easy for sure. The Lord is teaching us that this illness is simply a tool to teach us more about trusting Him. I often don't understand things, but every morning my dad reminds us that God is good and I believe it."

Sickness and disease tend to be very impersonal and far off until a friend or relative is in serious physical trouble. Cancer may become a daily issue. The care of an accident victim may change our plans for school. Heart disease may restrict activity and travel. The death of a family member may change everything. Illness and death are a very real part of life.

Megan and her family fought daily battles with her mother's illness. One day, unless the Lord dramatically intervenes, you will face a similar battle. Mark records many times when Jesus encountered either the ill or their friends and family. Jesus was able to view their conflict from God's perspective and also from man's. His actions and teachings help us to understand illness for what it is and then how to deal with it. His view may surprise you. As we believe and put His thoughts into practice, the Lord will prepare us for genuine victory when dealing with physical maladies. The length of this book will not permit an in-depth study of each situation. We can, however, examine a few key passages and start learning how Jesus responded to human illness.

Lessons at Peter's House
Mark 1:29-39

Mark continually shows us that Jesus kept a very busy schedule. Jesus started the day by teaching with great authority in the synagogue at Capernaum. He then cast out an unclean spirit from a man in the assembly. The news of these mighty deeds soon spread through all Galilee. Peter evidently invited Him to his home for the customary Sabbath meal, which was much like our Sunday dinner. The disciples told Jesus about Peter's mother-in-law and her fever. He entered her room, took her by the hand, and raised her up. The fever departed and she began to minister to them. Perhaps she prepared the meal. She took no medicines. There was not a period of convalescence. In the privacy of Peter's home, Jesus completely healed this woman.

Mark does not record the specific reactions of the people in the house. We can assume that they were utterly astonished. Not only could Jesus teach with great power, but His simple touch could heal sickness. The Jewish traditions of the day prescribed a remedy for this ailment. A person would tie an iron knife to a thorn bush using a lock of hair. He would then repeat certain Old Testament verses and cut down the bush. Christ's power, compassion, and simplicity stood in stark contrast to the mystical treatments of the rabbis.

Jesus immediately became the focus of attention in Peter's house and in all Capernaum. The people heard Him teach in the morning and heard that He healed a fever in the afternoon. At the end of the Sabbath day when people could travel, they started bringing the sick and diseased to Peter's door. Jesus healed each one. The variety of medical problems did not impede His work. Mark does not tell us how Jesus did it. His compassionate care may have extended well into the night.

The next paragraph reveals more of Jesus' purposes (Mark 1:35-39). The phrase "a great while before morning" refers to the fourth watch of the night or between 3 and 6 A.M. Jesus hid Himself outside the city in order to pray. Peter finally found Him and reported that the multitudes also looked for Him. Most teachers or healers would rejoice in such an enthusiastic following, but Jesus did not. It seems that for the time His work was completed in Capernaum. His desire and passion was to preach the gospel of the kingdom: man must repent of sins and believe. The miraculous healings gave credibility to the message of Christ. The physical need became the path to the spiritual opportunity. As God, Jesus knew that man's sin problem had eternal consequences. Man's physical problems are of this world. Although healing the body helped for a short while, preaching the gospel could save man forever. "And he preached in their synagogues throughout all Galilee, and cast out devils" (Mark 1:39). This verse directs our attention to Christ's routine of preaching and dealing with other needs.

World Religions and Medicine

HISTORICAL LIGHT

The connection between medical practice and religion has persisted from ancient civilizations to modern times. Encyclopedias and medical books contain many fascinating and sometimes grotesque accounts of medical procedures.

Mesopotamia: Priests examined animal and human intestines to manipulate spirits that caused illness. Hammurabi's law code specified severe punishments for doctors who failed to heal their patients. A surgeon whose patient died could have his hand cut off.

India: The Vedas, sacred Hindu writings, prescribed magical practices and incantations to remove demons that caused disease and other disorders. Surgeons used alcoholic drinks to ease pain and tar to seal incisions.

China: Chinese medical practices centered on the balance and control of yin and yang in the body. Like other things, the body consisted of wood, fire, earth, metal, and water. Careful interpretation of the pulse could determine the state of health and could predict the date of death. Herbal remedies and acupuncture helped maintain physical balances.

Greece: Asclepius, god of medicine, reportedly could heal those who came to his temples for baths and sleep. As the patients slept and dreamed, Asclepius gave them some particular cure. Hippocrates, the father of modern medicine, used honey as a primary medical treatment. He also drilled holes into people's heads to relieve pressure and sickness.

Lessons with a Leper
Mark 1:40-45

Leprosy—or Hansen's disease, as it is known today—is an affliction that most of us have not seen. Modern medical researchers believe that infected people spread the disease through discharges from the nose and mouth. Numbness, skin discoloration, and severe disfiguration may not appear for years after the initial infection. Doctors discovered the first effective drug treatment for leprosy in the 1940s. Most cases today occur in very poor areas of the world.

People in the ancient world dreaded leprosy and took significant action to restrain its spread. The Old Testament contains information on diagnosing and controlling it. Lepers were ceremonially unclean and were to be isolated from the rest of the Israelites according to Leviticus 13 and 14. Rabbis called leprosy "walking death" and had no cures for it. One rabbi said that he kept a separation of at least six feet from any leper and one hundred feet if the leper was upwind. He also threw rocks at them to keep them away. Most people associated leprosy with sin and the effects of sin.

Bible scholars do not know how many lepers lived in Palestine during Jesus' ministry. Based on general references in the New Testament and in other literature at the time, Jesus presumably saw lepers fairly often. They probably avoided Him as they would avoid the rabbis and other people.

Mark's account of Jesus' meeting with the leper is remarkable. It shows us Jesus' compassion for the sick. This man's focus on Christ reveals his faith. He had evidently seen or heard about Jesus' power to heal people. The leper approached Christ, knelt down, and humbly asked to be cleansed. He acknowledged Christ's power and desired His mercy. Christ touched him and said, "I will; be thou clean." The religious leaders and common people would never touch a leper for fear of contamination. Touching a leper would also make the individual ceremonially unclean. As the Son of God, Jesus' touch removed the defilement and immediately created a bond of compassion and comfort with the man. The healing was immediate.

The next verses show Jesus' intense compassion for this leper. Remember that the healings drew great crowds. Many wanted physical relief more than they wanted spiritual instruction. As God, Jesus knew man's inward motives, and He knew what this cleansed leper would do. The Greek verb translated "straitly charged" comes from a root that means "snort like a horse." Horses snort when they want to get someone's attention and when they want to communicate something very serious. Jesus told the healed man to do two things. First, he was not to tell anyone about the cleansing. From that we can assume that they were alone. Jesus worked quietly in this situation. He did not want the crowds thronging him for healing. Second, the man was to follow Moses' law for the ceremonial declaration of cleansing from leprosy. He should show himself to "the priest." The definite article with *priest* indicates that this was the high priest in Jerusalem. The high priest would certainly ask about the remarkable healing and the man could offer a specific testimony of Christ's power. By this time in Jesus' ministry, the religious leadership in Jerusalem opposed Him. The testimony of the cleansed leper would remind these people that Jesus was no ordinary teacher. It would also show them that Jesus wanted to confirm the law. The man departed and told everyone what Jesus had done for him. Jesus could no longer enter the city and preach the gospel due to the notoriety. As a man, Jesus' empathy and compassion for the hopeless leper led to the cleansing. Jesus would not turn away this man with such a great need and with equally great faith.

Lessons with a Leader
Mark 5:21-24, 35-43

The account of Jairus's daughter provides additional insight into Jesus' attitude about sickness and death. Your literature instructor may teach you to analyze a story for the meaning or for the author's purpose in writing it. When analyzing this story, we see that Jesus is certainly the main character. Some may assert

that the second primary character is the little girl. Notice, however, that the girl is entirely passive relative to the details provided by Mark. She was sick and later died. The most dynamic details concern Jairus himself. Jesus' words to him, "Be not afraid, only believe," seem to be the point of the narrative. Faith is not an end in itself. Faith builds a relationship between God and man. The infirmity of the daughter is the means or the tool that Jesus uses to strengthen Jairus's faith.

Let's examine some of the details. Jesus had just returned from a trip to Gadara on the other side of the Sea of Galilee. Huge crowds met him on the shore, which indicates that His popularity with the common people continued to grow. Jairus, a ruler of the synagogue, met Him with a most urgent request. In Mark 3:22, Jewish leaders had traveled to Galilee from Jerusalem and accused Jesus of working for Satan. Jairus, due to his rank, may have been aware of this accusation. But he also knew about Jesus' power to heal. The desperate condition of his daughter compelled him to break through the crowds and ask Jesus to heal her. Notice Jairus's emotion as recorded by his words "little daughter" and "point of death." The Greek grammar indicates that Jesus immediately departed with him and that the multitudes continually hindered their progress. Jairus's joy concerning Jesus' decision was quickly dashed by the delay with the woman. We will examine her case later. News came that the daughter had died. We can assume from human experience that Jairus lost all hope. Jesus encouraged him to believe and continued the journey. Professional mourners with their howls and shrieks of grief met them at the house.

Jesus communicated His intention to help the girl and they scornfully laughed at Him. Jairus's actions show that he believed Jesus. The mourners did not believe and were thus expelled from the house. Jesus touched the little girl as He had touched the leper. He then uttered "Talitha cumi," a common phrase in the everyday Aramaic language that means "Daughter, arise." These may have been the same words used by Jewish mothers when

Typical synagogue

Ministering to the Sick

Following Christ's example means, in part, ministering to the sick. You have a great opportunity to help people in your own age group. Fear is the main reason that Christians fail in this area. As a teen, always seek the advice of a parent or spiritual leader before proceeding. Ask about the person's needs and then formulate a plan to help. Something as simple as a friendly chat or gathering homework assignments can be great encouragement. Every situation is different, so flexibility is vital. Always try to communicate God's Word and show compassion.

waking their children from sleep in the morning. Mark's inclusion of the specific phrase points to the deep impression that the words made on the hearers. Christ's touch and words raised a girl from the dead. The people in the house were astonished. We get the English word *ecstasy* from Mark's description of their reaction. Their joy and delight over the daughter's new life led to a deeper relationship with the Christ, the source of all life. Jesus told them not to spread the details around the community so that He could continue His preaching ministry. He also asked them to give the girl something to eat. Even in the smallest details, Jesus showed His compassion for those in need.

Lessons with a Lady
Mark 5:24-34

We might say that Jairus's faith was initially weak and many enemies attacked it. In the end, his faith in Christ prevailed, and his daughter's life was restored. Mark records another incident, which Jairus saw. Again, the chief issue seems to be faith, or trust. Superstition and fear melted when Jesus said, "Daughter, thy faith hath made thee whole; go in peace, and be whole of thy plague" (Mark 5:34).

Hospital visits can be especially scary. Here are some suggestions to help:

1. Do not visit alone. Enlist the help of a friend or family member.

2. Stop at the visitors' information desk and ask about specific regulations and guidelines for your visit. Obeying the rules will help you to gain the respect of the medical professionals and will make the visit easier.

3. Keep the visit fairly short. Ask the patient to tell you when he or she is tired or when you should leave the room for other reasons.

4. End the visit if the patient is in severe pain, is being actively treated, or is eating. Assure him that you will come back at a more appropriate time.

5. Don't try to help with medical procedures. Summon the hospital staff for the need.

6. Remember that you are God's servant and that your purpose is to show compassion and concern. Be cheerful and positive.

7. Ask if you can pray with your friend before departing. Be brief and specific.

8. Ask if you can take care of some need outside the hospital. Follow through on anything reasonable that is asked.

9. Set up another time when you can visit the patient either in the hospital or at home.

10. Always wash your hands after exiting the hospital building.

The longest sentence in Mark's Gospel describes the condition of the lady with an issue of blood. A good way to understand a complicated sentence is to find the simple subject, the verb, and then the object. The other parts will be understood as modifying one of the essential parts. In Mark 5:25-27, the basic sentence with a few modifiers included for clarity is, "A woman touched his garment."

The intervening words communicate her history. Her name and specific identity are not given. She may have been a stranger to the folks in the town. According to Leviticus 15:25-27, those in her condition were ceremonially unclean, along with anyone who touched them. It seems reasonable that after so many years of illness, people would know of her situation and would demand her separation from the crowds. The woman tried everything possible to heal the affliction. The Talmud, a collection of Jewish traditions, records eleven different remedies to stop an issue of blood. Perhaps the local doctors used one or more of these treatments. Nothing worked and she became worse. Upon hearing about Jesus, the woman traveled to the town and worked her way through the crowds in order to touch His garment. "If I may touch but his clothes, I shall be whole"—this is the verbal expression of a faith that takes action. After coming to Him from behind, she touched Christ's outer robe. Immediately the bleeding ceased.

At this point in the narrative, most of us would conclude that the woman's problem was solved and that Jesus could now help Jairus. Jesus looked at the situation much differently. He wanted to perfect her faith and rid it of harmful elements. Jesus stopped and asked, "Who touched my clothes?" The disciples thought that His question was ridiculous since the crowd pressed upon Him. Jesus continued to look for the woman until she came and confessed her actions. The text implies that she told Him the whole story of her affliction. Jesus addresses her as "daughter" which implies a close relationship. He reinforces the concept of a relationship by telling her that her faith, not the superstitious touching of a piece of cloth, healed her. Many ancient remedies used rituals and enchantments. His search for her led to the personal relationship that was much more important than the physical healing. The phrase "go in peace" might better be translated "go into peace," which indicates a much brighter future for the woman than she could imagine before her meeting with Jesus. The text also indicates that while Jesus spoke to her, the message arrived about Jairus's daughter. The attention of the crowd turned away from her, thus protecting her privacy. She could enjoy her newfound health without questions from the crowd. Once again, Jesus showed compassion even in the smallest details.

Fanny Crosby: Blind Yet Believing

Fanny Crosby (1820-1915) lost her sight as an infant when a phony doctor prescribed the wrong ointment for an eye problem. She later attended and taught at the New York Institute for the Blind. A cholera epidemic struck the city and the school in 1849. Many students died. The tragedies made Fanny realize that she knew about God, but did not know God personally. She trusted Christ at a revival meeting. A few years later, sorrow once again visited when her only child died in infancy.

Sickness and sorrow often make people bitter and resentful against God. Fanny Crosby's poetry reveals her unfailing faith in God's goodness and sovereignty. Great human affliction and sorrow became God's tool to fill Christian hymnals with songs of praise. Notice that Fanny Crosby emphasizes the Lord's character and grace in her popular "All the Way My Savior Leads Me."

All the way my Savior leads me;
What have I to ask beside?
Can I doubt His tender mercy,
Who through life has been my Guide?
Heavenly peace, divinest comfort,
Here by faith in Him to dwell!
For I know, whate'er befall me,
Jesus doeth all things well.

All the way my Savior leads me,
Cheers each winding path I tread,
Gives me grace for every trial,
Feeds me with the living bread.
Though my weary steps may falter
And my soul athirst may be,
Gushing from the Rock before me,
Lo! A spring of joy I see.

All the way my Savior leads me;
Oh, the fullness of His love!
Perfect rest to me is promised
In my Father's house above.
When my spirit, clothed immortal,
Wings its flight to realms of day,
This my song through endless ages:
Jesus led me all the way.

Our Situation Today

Let's review what we have learned about Jesus' ministry to the sick. At Peter's home, Jesus proved that He had the power to heal all types of illness. His actions, however, showed that His priority was not the healing of the body but the saving of the soul through preaching. The miracles of healing gave visual and powerful credibility to His messages in the synagogues. The incident with the leper in Galilee showed Christ's enormous compassion for the physical needs of man. His care and power contrasted with the hatefulness of the religious leaders of that time. In Jairus's case, we see Jesus not only dealing with the death of a child but also strengthening the weak faith of a very religious man. The woman with the issue of blood had faith, but it was marred by superstition.

Christ healed her body and purified her faith. Mark records nine specific people that Jesus healed. He also shows us in four passages that Jesus' normal routine included curing sickness of every sort. Relieving human suffering played an important part in Christ's ministry.

God in His wisdom provided us with details of Christ's life so that we might understand His thinking about our lives. Learning Christ's lessons on illness will bring great peace and quietness during difficult times, which are certain to come. Let's first remember the theological purpose of Christ's healing ministry. His actions contrasted with the dead religion of the day and pointed to

Medicines in the Bible

The Bible is a book of theology. Medical issues support God's communication to us but are not a main focus of the Scriptures. The Lord can certainly heal our sicknesses, but He expects us to use appropriate means for physical health. Most of us are very thankful for adequate healthcare and modern medicines. Look up the following verses and state the treatment being used.

Proverbs 17:22 _____

Isaiah 1:6 _____

Isaiah 38:21 _____

Jeremiah 8:22 _____

Ezekiel 47:12 _____

Luke 10:34 _____

I Timothy 5:23 _____

the fact that He was the Messiah. Only God had such great power over the worst diseases and even over death. "Surely he hath borne our griefs, and carried our sorrows" (Isaiah 53:4) may refer to Christ's healing ministry. Just as Christ could heal physical sickness, so we may be confident that He can dismiss the power of sin. His actions give credibility to both His person and His words.

Other purposes of Christ's healing seem to center on a fuller relationship with God. The miracles were never an end in themselves. Sinners saw Christ's great power and many were more eager to hear Him as a result. Many people will not consider spiritual truth until their body fails. Believers often realize their utter dependence upon God when cancer or disease develops. Our physical problems must point us toward greater dependence upon God. Illness does not communicate God's displeasure but rather His everlasting love. The unsaved see life as an end in itself, but Christians look forward to eternal fellowship with God in heaven. If sickness and disease can draw me closer to God, then I can face the malady with a bright hope of better times possibly on earth and certainly in heaven.

As representatives of Christ, we can and should follow His example in dealing with the sick. Christians cannot heal people the way Christ did. We can, however, show compassion by specific acts of kindness and concern. If the purpose of sickness is to cultivate a better relationship to God, then presenting God's Word to those in need must be a priority. Believers can also assure those in need that God does indeed love them. Focusing on the eternal results of physical illness gives us the tool to handle the troublesome days that illness may bring.

Review Questions

A. Greece
B. Fever
C. Jesus
D. Vedas
E. Fanny Crosby

F. Hansen's disease
G. Jewish writings
H. Howl
I. Ruler
J. Meeting place

_____ 1. Mother-in-law

_____ 2. Asclepius

_____ 3. Jairus

_____ 4. Talmud

_____ 5. Messiah

_____ 6. India

_____ 7. Leprosy

_____ 8. Mourner

_____ 9. Blind

_____ 10. Synagogue

11. Why did Jesus leave Capernaum in Mark 1?

12. How did Jesus' approach to healing differ from that of pagan religions?

13. Why would a leper be considered "unclean"?

14. What obstacles did Jairus's faith overcome in Mark 5?

15. In what way was the woman with the issue of blood exercising a superstitious faith?

Christ and the Forces of Evil

4

Reuben Mason rested on one knee as sweat dripped down his face and soaked his gym shirt. The university gym seemed unusually hot that day. The physical education teacher blew the whistle signaling the end of that wrestling match and the beginning of the next. Reuben knew that his turn to wrestle the largest and strongest guy in the class would come in just a few minutes. His mind wandered back to about three years earlier when he had had to take wrestling in high school. The very same thing had happened. On the last day of class, the teacher organized a tournament. He drew names from a bag to determine the first-round opponents. Reuben's adversary was huge. The match lasted exactly twenty-eight seconds. He could not remember whether he had been happier that the match was over or that he endured for so long. It could have been over much sooner.

The shrill whistle jarred Reuben's mind back to the task at hand. As the guys approached the center of the mat, the coach reminded them of the rules. Just before the action started, one of Reuben's friends yelled out, "I'm glad it's you and not me!"

Reuben quickly retorted, "Look at the tournament board. You get the winner of this round!"

This time, the match lasted fifteen seconds. Reuben's opponent went on to crush everyone else in the class. No one stood much of a chance against this big, strong guy who enjoyed wrestling. Reuben was greatly relieved that wrestling class was over. He just hoped that the coach would be merciful and give him a C for the semester.

Like Reuben, I had to take wrestling for a required physical education course. The coach talked a lot about being big, strong, and fast. I quickly learned that I was neither big nor strong nor fast. You can guess the results: at the time, I did not like the class at all.

In retrospect, the Lord taught me a lot through wrestling. I learned about my personal weakness in wrestling with a strong foe called *sin*. Most Christians will recognize that rebellion against God is everywhere, including inside us. All too often, we commit sin, which is just like being pinned in wrestling class. It controls and defeats us. Jesus knows about the problem. The Gospel of Mark shows us Jesus' wrestling match with the representatives of sin and gives us a strategy to defeat them.

You know from studying history or government that the president or king often acts on behalf of an entire nation. This powerful person speaks for and represents all the people. We will see Christ our leader as He fights Satan's armies that represent sin and rebellion. Jesus defeated sin, and we can too as we learn from Him. In this chapter, we will first look at Christ's explanation of the battle and then at four examples of His victory. In each case, we will see the power of Christ over evil. We will then examine the basics of a relationship with Christ that guarantees victory for us.

Basics of the Battle
Mark 3:22-30

Christ's conversation with the scribes in Mark 3 occurred toward the middle of His ministry. Great crowds from all over Palestine had heard about Jesus and wanted to see Him (Mark 3:7, 8). The religious leadership in Jerusalem did not like what they were hearing and did not like the fact that so many people followed Jesus. They devised a plan to discredit His ministry, which might destroy His popularity.

To the great amazement of the crowds, Jesus cast unclean spirits, or demons, out of people. Some of the scribes came to Galilee and began to tell people that Jesus had an unclean spirit and that He cast out unclean spirits through the power of Beelzebub (Mark 3:22, 30). In order to understand this slander, let's first examine their terminology. *Unclean* means dirty or filthy. When applied to religious matters, it means that something is totally void of moral purity or value. We should also understand that the word spirit did not refer to an emotion or a personality trait. When someone enthusiastically cheers for his team, we may say that he has "spirit." But in this context, the word refers to an evil being that followed Satan in rebellion against God. While the origin of these evil beings is not certain, they are obviously evil and devoted to harming humankind.

Notice also the slanderous intent behind the scribes' use of the word *Beelzebub*. The term can mean "lord of the flies," and is associated with human and animal refuse. It may also mean "lord of the dwelling." In Jewish teaching, this evil being was the chief of the devils. The scribes wanted to associate Jesus with the emissaries of evil in order to achieve their own selfish purposes.

Jesus did not let the wicked accusations go unchallenged. His graceful response shows us the nature of the battle against evil. In Mark 3:23-26, Jesus told the scribes and the people that evil has unity of purpose and has one leader. The leader is Satan, who constantly opposes God and works against the spiritual success of mankind. His name means "adversary." Jesus reminded them that a divided kingdom or house will come to ruin. What would happen if someone on your basketball team started playing for the other side? The coach would promptly remove that person from the game and from the team. Likewise, governments execute spies for working for the enemy. Companies dismiss workers who help the competition. Jesus' words certainly imply that His actions destroy Satan's domination of men. Simply stated, Christ performed the will of God by casting out the unclean spirits and by freeing men from sin's domination. The accusation of the scribes is completely illogical even to the least educated.

Christ not only pointed out the error of scribes, He also explained His function in the battle. In Mark 3:27, notice Christ's graciousness in the story of the strong man. Jesus never said that Beelzebub is the strong man, but that is certainly the assumption based on the derivation of the name. Christ did clearly state that He is stronger than the strong man, which implies His deity. He gave the people the truth they required without exalting Himself and without needlessly offending them. Three actions characterize Christ's domination of evil. He enters the strong man's house, binds him, and then takes his possessions. Christ entered the domain of evil at His birth and more particularly when His public ministry began. Christ also silenced and controlled the unclean spirits, which points to their binding. The fact that Jesus freed people from unclean spirits indicates the spoiling of Satan's possessions. The matchless power of Christ defeats even the worst examples of evil.

One additional thought must also be noted. The scribes accused Jesus of unthinkable evil. Jesus kindly refuted them. He then pointed out the seriousness of their sin before God.

Flavius Josephus: Jewish Historian

HISTORICAL LIGHT

Josephus (A.D. 37-100) spent his early years studying Jewish religion. He later traveled to Rome to ask Nero

for the freedom of two priests. While there, he learned about the Roman government and way of life. After returning to Palestine, he supported Jewish freedom fighters and saw the destruction of Herod's temple. A military commander then sent Josephus to Rome as a prisoner. Once released, he wrote several large books detailing the history of the Jews for the benefit of the Romans. The following excerpt shows a Jewish remedy that uses a tree root to cure demon possession.

"There is a certain place called Baaras, which produces a root of the same name with itself; its colour is like to that of flame, and towards the evening it sends out a certain ray like lightning: it is not easily taken by such as would do it, but recedes from their hands, nor will yield itself to be taken quietly. They dig a trench quite around it, till the hidden part be very small, then they tie a dog to it, and when the dog tries hard to follow him that tied him, this root is easily plucked up, but the dog dies immediately, as if it were instead the man that would take the plant away. Yet, after all this pains in getting it, it is only valuable on account of one virtue it hath, that if it be brought to sick persons, it quickly drives away those called Demons, which are no other than the spirits of the wicked, which enter into men that are alive, and kill them, unless they can obtain some help against them" (Josephus, *Wars of the Jews*, Book 7, Chapter 6, paragraph 3).

Attributing Christ's power to an evil spirit, or blasphemy against the Holy Spirit, is a sin so heinous that God will not forgive it. Jesus implied that these seemingly righteous men had no fellowship with God. By rejecting Christ, they cut themselves off from the source of true life and are now swallowed up in the realm of evil.

Some people worry that they may have committed this sin. There is no need for God's children to worry. At the heart of blasphemy against the Holy Spirit is a total hatred of God. Because those who worry about this sin show tenderness for the things of God, they have certainly not committed the unpardonable sin.

Victory at Capernaum
Mark 1:23-28

Jesus' great preaching ministry brought Him to the synagogue at Capernaum. The people wondered at His teaching because it was so unlike the contradictory doctrines of the religious leaders. Mark tells us that the congregation included a man with an unclean spirit. The very fact that such a person would attend Sabbath services pointed to the deadness of the people's religion and understanding. Perhaps they did not recognize the man's true problem, or they may have lacked the power to do anything about it. The man with the unclean spirit immediately recognized Jesus and exclaimed, "What have we to do with thee?" The literal Greek translation is "what to us and to you," meaning that the two parties have nothing in common. The evil spirit thinks that Jesus came from Nazareth to Capernaum to ruin him. As the Holy One of God, Jesus' control of the unclean spirit was absolute.

Mark tells us that Jesus rebuked him. The term *rebuke* points to Jesus' superiority over the unclean spirit. A school principal may rebuke a student for poor grades, but a student would never rebuke a principal. Two things about the unclean spirit must change. First, he must hold his peace or be quiet. The Greek verb literally means "be muzzled." Just as a pet owner puts a muzzle onto a dog to keep it from biting or barking, so Christ silenced any testimony about Himself from the unclean spirit. Only holy beings have the liberty to publicly exalt a holy God. He also told the spirit to come out of the man. The power and nature of Christ compelled the spirit to obey. The man's convulsions and cry proved to the onlookers that the unclean spirit actually departed.

The people in the synagogue reacted with utter amazement at Jesus' power. The religious leaders performed elaborate ceremonies and prescribed medicines to remove demons. Jesus was something new. Evidently, intense discussions broke out about the events in the synagogue. News spread quickly throughout the region. Just who was this man, and how could he have such great power? We know that this man was God's Son, the Messiah of Israel. Mark begins his Gospel with a simple declaration about Christ's person and then proceeds to show us the events that prove Jesus' claims of deity. Christians trust all that Jesus said and did. But we know from Mark that many of the people who saw and heard Jesus never really believed him. They instead wondered and talked about Him. Most seemed glad for the benefits of healing and for the removal of unclean spirits, but they never repented and trusted. Experiences must lead to Christ. Real victory over evil in our lives begins when we move beyond the experience and into a trusting relationship with Christ.

Victory at Gadara
Mark 5:1-20

Jesus' next major battle with evil took place on the Sea of Galilee's east bank in the region known as Gadara. The Romans built ten Greek-style cities in the area. The new Roman and Greek culture attracted many Jews who retained their Jewish nationality but who also enjoyed the corrupt pagan practices and prosperity. Most Jews from Judea despised these people for their relation-

ship to the Romans. The strange mix of religions and cultures made a great place for Jesus to teach us about Himself and His power.

We can only imagine what the disciples thought as they stepped off the boat onto the shore of this wicked place and saw a demon-possessed man running toward them from the tombs. Mark's detailed description of the man probably reflects Peter's fear. But notice this man's subjection to Jesus in Mark 5:6, 7. He ran to Jesus, worshiped Him, and then begged Him for a reprieve from torment. Jesus asked the demon's name for the benefit of the disciples. A legion was a powerful, well-equipped army of about six thousand Roman soldiers. The emperor used many legions to conquer the world and to maintain control over unruly provinces like Judea. Jesus stood face to face with a great army of demons and, by simply speaking, He cast them out of the man. The demons asked Jesus to allow them to enter a herd of hogs that were feeding near the mountains. Old Testament law prohibited the Jews from eating pork and so it's possible that the owners of the pigs were disobedient Jews. Jesus granted their request to prove that He had removed the demons from the man and to prick the conscience of the Jews in the area. When the demons entered the animals, they immediately ran over a cliff, fell into the sea, and were drowned. Even in a hostile place when confronted by hordes of unclean spirits, the Son of God demonstrated His power over evil and His compassion for man.

The next skirmish in the battle shows us two very different reactions to Christ's power. Like messengers at a battle, the pig keepers ran through the region and reported the news to everyone. The crowd came and saw not only Jesus, but also the man who was now perfectly normal. Mark tells us that the people reacted with fear and wanted Jesus to leave. Ancient pagans often feared unknown spiritual powers. Jesus represented a threat to their religion. Or maybe they were upset about the economic consequences of losing the pigs.

In either case, they preferred to be left alone, and Jesus departed from them. Observe now the request of the man who had been freed from the demons. He wanted to be with Jesus. Christ announced different plans for this man. Since the people had rejected Christ's personal ministry to them, He would now send one of their own to testify of the truth. The man obediently departed and told everyone about Jesus' power and compassion. These responses near the Sea of Galilee occur all over the world today. Some will reject Christ for various reasons. Others will obediently believe Him. We can evaluate our personal relationship to God based on our response to Christ's power and compassion.

Victory at Tyre and Sidon
Mark 7:24-30

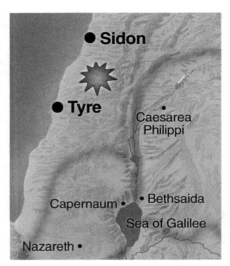

After Jesus finished rebuking the religious leaders, He decided to travel toward Tyre and Sidon. He probably wanted to get away from Galilee in order to teach the disciples in private and to get some rest. These two well-known Roman seaports were infused with Gentile culture. Elijah had stayed with a widow and her son in this area, and God miraculously sustained them with meal and oil for a long time. In this spiritually dark place, Jesus showed His power over evil and showed the surprising faith of a Gentile woman.

Jesus quietly entered a house, but Mark 7:25 records that somehow, a Gentile woman whose daughter had an unclean spirit knew about Jesus and found Him at the house. In typical oriental fashion, she fell at His feet, signifying submission, and asked Jesus to cast out her daughter's unclean spirit. The fact that the daughter was in another location points to the woman's great faith. Jesus then acted to further expose her faith for our encouragement. "Let the children first be filled: for it is not meet to take the children's bread and cast it unto the dogs" reflected a common household scene. Small pet dogs sat under the kitchen table looking for scraps or crumbs that fell to the floor. Jesus gently reminded her that His ministry was primarily to the Jews and that her lowly position as a Gentile did not entitle her to the request. The woman's wise response acknowledged Jesus' mission to the Jews, but pointed out that Christ's abundance was plenty for all. Jesus rewarded her faith by granting the request. He completely removed the unclean spirit from the daughter, which brought about a state of rest for both the mother and the girl. The mother's persistent and wise faith enabled Christ to display His power and compassion.

Spiritual Warfare

PRINCIPLES APPLIED

John Bunyan (1628-1688) spent about twelve years in an English prison for preaching the gospel of Christ. The prison cell restricted his movements but could not restrict his zeal for God. Bunyan wrote *The Pilgrim's Progress*, an allegorical story about the Christian life, as well as eleven other books. The following selection chronicles Christian's battle with Apollyon, the evil ruler of this world. Notice the weapon Christian uses to defeat his enemy.

> Then Apollyon, espying his opportunity, began to gather up close to Christian, and wrestling with him, gave him a dreadful fall; and with that, Christian's sword flew out of his hand. Then said Apollyon, I am sure of thee now. And with that he had almost pressed him to death; so that Christian began to despair of life: but as God would have it, while Apollyon was fetching of his last blow, thereby to make a full end of this good man, Christian nimbly stretched out his hand for his sword, and caught it, saying, "Rejoice not against me, O mine enemy: when I fall, I shall arise" (Micah 7:8); and with that gave him a deadly thrust, which made him give back, as one that had received his mortal wound. Christian perceiving that, made at him again, saying, "Nay, in all these things we are more than conquerors through Him that loved us" (Rom. 8:37).

> And with that Apollyon spread forth his dragon's wings, and sped him away, that Christian for a season saw him no more (James 4:7).

Victory at Caesarea Philippi
Mark 9:14-29

Jesus had just returned with Peter, James, and John from the mountain of transfiguration. Any doubts about Christ's deity should have been settled for the three disciples. They had seen Jesus in His glory and heard the affirming voice of God the Father about His Son. Upon entering an area around the city, they saw and heard the scribes interrogating the disciples about their inability to cast out an unclean spirit from a boy. It's ironic that the scribes who could not help this man and his son would question someone else for trying. Jesus asked them about the debate, and the father related the boy's condition. Again we see Christ's unchallenged power. At the appropriate moment, He simply commanded the spirit to depart and ministered to the boy's remaining

weakness. What the disciples could not do, Jesus accomplished with ease. God's power always vanquishes evil.

Jesus used this event to teach both the father and the disciples several important lessons. Let's consider the father's situation first. The fact that he was desperate for help is obvious from the long description of his son's affliction. Jesus invited the father to tell Him even more by asking when the problem had started. The father answered with more information and with a plea. "But if thou canst do any thing, have compassion on us, and help us" shows faith, but the faith needs to mature. He questioned the power of Christ instead of acknowledging his own deficiency. Jesus exposed the real issue with His answer. He used the father's own words to show him the need for strong faith. When the father confessed his weakness, Jesus granted the request. The healed son would constantly remind the father of two vital principles: sinful man is weak and Christ is strong and compassionate.

Secondly, Jesus had a lesson for the disciples. He rebuked the crowd, and the disciples in particular, by calling them a "faithless generation." After the son was restored, the disciples asked Jesus why they could not cast out the unclean spirit. Jesus told them that this situation required a close relationship with God cultivated through prayer and fasting. Some situations are humanly more difficult than others. The disciples could handle the tough problems only as they drew closer to God. Notice, however, that the words of Christ crushed the most difficult problems with evil.

Victory for Us

Mark gives us four detailed accounts in which Jesus defeated the representatives of sin and showed great compassion for man. The locations and circumstances differed, but the power of Christ was always the same. Jesus displayed His power and authority to teach us important spiritual lessons. Some wondered at His power but never really believed. Others asked Jesus to depart, and He granted their shortsighted request. But Jesus acted to strengthen the faith of those who truly believed. They enjoyed the freedom and victory of knowing the Son of God.

You are probably very familiar with the story of David and Goliath. The Philistine giant wanted to fight the champion of

Israel to determine the winner of the war between the two countries. Goliath's size and strength scared even the most experienced soldiers of Israel. One day, David heard the giant's threats and blasphemies. The young shepherd boy found some smooth stones and used his sling to hurl one of them right between the giant's eyes. Goliath died at David's hand. The Israelites chased and defeated the Philistine armies. Just as David, the representative of Israel, defeated the giant, so Christ our representative defeated the powers of evil when He cast out unclean spirits.

The Apostle Paul writes often about believers being "in Christ," which seems to be a difficult concept to understand. But, from the Gospel of Mark, we see that Christ defeated Satan at every battle. My biggest problem is not physical health, mental weakness, lack of money, or other people. The inward struggle with my sinful heart is my most difficult and persistent problem. If you have trusted Christ as your Savior, you have the same struggles. Being "in Christ" means that He has won the victory over evil for me. I cannot do it for myself. Only the all-powerful Son of God can defeat the enemy of my soul. My part is to believe that I win through Jesus and then to chase the enemies out of my heart. Most of us will have doubts and fears about God's dealings in our lives from time to time. The best weapon against such assaults is to remember God's goodness to us in the past and then to find His comforting promises to us in the Bible. Modern technology continually presents evil to us through television, newspapers, radio, and the Internet. We may need to guard our hearts by avoiding or restricting these conduits of rebellion against God. We will never completely win the battle against wickedness in this world. Mark 16:19 tells us that Christ "was received up into heaven, and sat on the right hand of God." Because believers are in Christ, one day we too will sit with Christ in heaven, far away from the pollution of this evil world. I look forward to that day and hope that you do as well.

Roman Armor and Christian Battle

HISTORICAL
LIGHT

The apostle Paul sat in a Roman prison chained to a soldier. Probably as a result of Julius Caesar's murder, the Roman emperors had decided to keep the best legions close to the capital for protection. The soldier's armor inspired Paul's thoughts about the believer's warfare with evil. Believers today can stand against every type of evil by using the Christian soldier's armor. Are you prepared for the battle?

Head:
Salvation
Helmet of iron and bronze

Chest:
Righteousness
Breastplate made of over-
lapping metal plates

Weapon:
Word of God.
18 in. long double-edged
sword used for thrusting

Loins:
God's Truth
Leather belt

Whole body:
Faith
Shield made of wood over-
laid with metal and deco-
rated according to the legion

Feet:
Gospel
(witnessing)
Multi-layered sandals with
straps up to mid shin

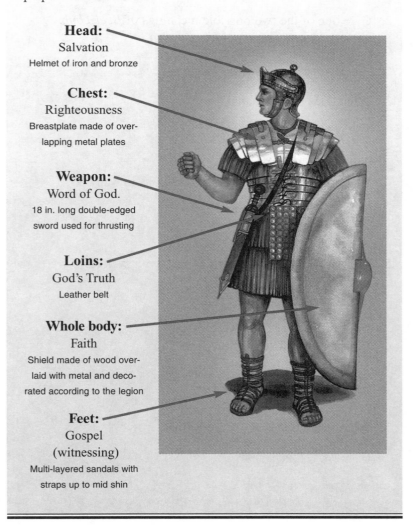

Review Questions

1. What religious group opposed Christ's ministry in Galilee?

2. Give one of the two possible meanings of *Beelzebub*.

3. What does Satan's name mean?

4. Who took the strong man's possessions in Mark 3?

5. What is the literal meaning of *hold your peace?*

6. Who wrote a history of the Jews?

7. What is the name of a large Roman army?

8. Who fought with Christian in *The Pilgrim's Progress*?

9. What Gentile seaport towns did Jesus travel near?

10. What weapon does the Christian soldier use?

11. What did Jesus call His disciples and the crowd at Caesarea?

12. What did Jesus want the father in Caesarea to confess?

Essay

13. What did Jesus do to cast out unclean spirits?

14. Contrast Jesus' method of casting out unclean spirits with the Jews' methods.

15. Why did the hogs run into the sea?

16. How did unclean spirits show subjection to Christ?

17. Why were the disciples powerless to remove the unclean spirit near Caesarea?

18. Why did Jesus send the man who had been possessed by the legion back to his own country?

19. How did the woman near Tyre show submission to Christ?

20. What is the meaning of "in Christ"?

Christ and the Religious Leadership

5

Adam Nelson's and David Cummings's hearts raced faster as the bottom of the inning started. David hardly noticed his wet and sticky shirt. Their high school team, the Winchester Cougars, had tied the final game of the regular season with a home run in the last inning. They needed to keep the other team from scoring in order to put the game into extra innings.

Adam yelled, "I guess I need to buy you a soft drink since I knocked yours out of your hand and onto your shirt. I got a little excited when the ball flew over the fence!"

"If we win this game, I'll buy you a super-sized milk shake for putting up with all my cheering and screaming," answered David.

The first batter came to the plate and promptly struck out. Both guys jumped up and shouted approvingly to the team. They quickly sat down when the next guy hit a long double into right field. After walking the next batter, the pitcher looked tired, so the coach immediately brought in Phil Larson to finish the game. Phil had a perfect pitching record of four wins and no losses. He was the best man for the job. Adam and David started shouting along with the rest of the fans from Winchester.

Phil's first pitch was hit directly at the short stop for an easy second out. The next pitch hit the batter to load the bases. David said that the ball was supposed to curve, but for some reason it had not. Both guys seemed to have absolute confidence in Phil's pitching. After a brief conference between pitcher and catcher, the game resumed. Phil threw two quick strikes, and everybody stood to cheer. The next pitch flew over the catcher's head and hit the backstop! The game promptly ended when the runner at third base jogged home for the winning run.

As the guys walked out of the stadium, Adam mumbled, "This is absolutely my last baseball game."

David reassured him, "Don't be so gloomy! Everyone fails at one time or another. The whole team will play again next year, and we have a great shot at winning the state championship."

Adam shrugged his shoulders and walked quietly to the car. The guys did enjoy two very large milk shakes, and they laughed about the wet shirt. Neither said a word about baseball. It would be ten years before Adam would attend another game.

Most of us regularly deal with disappointments of one type or another. The death of a family member, a poor grade in a hard class, or the loss of a ball game can lead to emotional distress. One of the hardest situations for us to handle appropriately is improper behavior by religious leaders. We perceive that something is wrong, and then like Adam we decide to abandon everything related to the situation.

The consequences of such a decision can destroy our lives for both time and eternity. Others of us will maintain a respect for God, but will shun church and any contact with Christians out of the fear of being disappointed again. These people may know Christ as their Savior, but they fail to enjoy the life that God has planned for them. One of the big obstacles to Christian maturity is learning to recognize and deal with religious hypocrites and failures.

Even a cursory reading of Mark's Gospel reveals that Jesus often exposed the sin and weakness of the religious leadership in Israel. The common people gladly received Christ's teaching. Did these people realize that something was wrong with their leaders? Christ's words and actions attracted great multitudes because they saw in Jesus something better and something new. As deity, Jesus had the right to judge the deeds of a religion that supposedly pointed people to God. He also had the ability to explain God's Word so that people might repent and believe.

The religion of the day was man-oriented and failed to meet God's standards. Most of the leaders looked at Jesus as a threat to their way of life. In Mark 11:28, they asked Him, "By what authority doest thou these things? and who gave thee this authority to do these things?" They saw Christ's great power, but failed to understand His deity and His authority. Jesus' evaluation of these people is simple. At the end of His time on earth, Jesus told the disciples that "the Son of man is betrayed into the hands of sinners" (Mark 14:41). The "sinners" included the religious leaders in Jerusalem. Jesus did not let the failures and hostility of popular religion stop Him from doing the will of God. Neither should we. Mark presents to us the religious leadership's three different approaches to dealing with Christ. Each one reveals the superiority of knowing Christ personally over participating in failed religion. Understanding both the greatness of Christ and the foolishness of man's religion will insulate us from disappointments, which are certain to come.

Jewish Religious Groups of the First Century

Religious practices can be very confusing to people of differing times and cultures. Mark needed to explain even to the Romans the hand-washing rituals of the Pharisees. (See Mark 7:3, 4.) Background knowledge about Jewish religious practices and organizations will greatly enhance our understanding of the Gospels.

Pharisees: The Pharisees first organized about 150 B.C. as a reaction against heathen practices. Their name means "separate ones." According to Josephus, who was a Pharisee, the group had about six thousand members at the time of Christ. They believed the Old Testament law plus many oral traditions from rabbis through the years. Jesus rejected the oral traditions because they were merely the teachings of man. Strict separation from all pagan and heathen influence motivated many of the Pharisees' practices. Following the destruction of Jerusalem in A.D. 70, the Pharisees established a settlement near the Mediterranean Sea. Over the centuries Phariseeism developed into modern Orthodox Judaism.

Sadducees: The politically astute Sadducees were primarily upper-class priests who controlled temple worship and civil government. They believed in only the five books of Moses and rejected the Pharisees' oral traditions. Most did not believe in the resurrection or in anything supernatural. The Sadducees maintained their power by cooperating with the Romans. Most took Greek names. They ceased to exist as a group once the temple was destroyed.

The Period of Curiosity
Mark 2:1–3:6

This section records five separate confrontations between Christ and representatives from various religious groups. The conflict escalates from internal reasoning about Christ's actions (Mark 2:6) to questioning Jesus' disciples (Mark 2:16), to confronting Jesus about the actions of the disciples (Mark 2:24), and finally to plotting to kill Jesus (Mark 3:6). The scribes and Pharisees seemed to watch Jesus' every move. They wanted to learn more about Him, which seems very commendable on the surface. Jesus pointed out their weaknesses so that they might repent and believe. Regrettably, these men did not understand because they held onto religious tradition and practice.

Herodians: The Herodians are not known outside the New Testament. Their name suggests that the group was closely associated with King Herod. They may have believed that Herod was the best hope for a free Israel.

Essenes: The Essenes are not directly mentioned in the Gospels; however, Josephus and other historians attest to their existence. They withdrew from Jewish society in order to wait for the Messiah and to preserve the purity of their beliefs. Some archeologists believe that the Essenes had a village near Jerusalem and that Jesus entered the village to eat the Last Supper with His disciples.

Scribes: The scribes were not a political movement, but rather experts on the law. Many Pharisees were scribes. They made copies of the law and acted as the secretaries in meetings of the Sanhedrin.

Sanhedrin: The Sanhedrin was a governmental body of about seventy men who controlled Jewish political and religious affairs. In Christ's time, the high priest acted as president of the group. Most members were from wealthy families and included scribes and Sadducees. King Herod evidently favored the Pharisees and gave them seats on the council. This body tried and condemned Jesus. (See Mark 14:55 and 15:1.)

Many of you are familiar with the events in Mark 2:1-12. Four men carried a sick friend to Jesus. Since they could not come inside the house, they decided to go up to the roof, remove a section of it, and then lower their friend into Jesus' presence for healing.

Christ did heal this man, but more importantly, He taught us some important lessons about Himself. Mark records that faith reveals the power of God (Mark 2:5). The scribes looked to ritual and to traditional teachings for a relationship to God. Jesus first dealt with the sick man's sin, which was his most critical need. Perhaps the man feared that his personal sin caused the physical impairment. Maybe he had heard Jesus preaching about repentance and realized that he was a sinner like everyone else. The scribes reasoned correctly that only God could forgive sins, but they did not recognize that Jesus was God. Jesus gave them an illustrated lesson about His power over sin and about His deity when He restored the man's health. The physical healing pointed to the reality of the spiritual healing. The scribes could do neither.

Christ's next actions struck right at the heart of the most outwardly pious members of Jewish society. He called Levi, or Matthew, a tax collector, to be one of His disciples. He then attended a dinner with Levi's associates who were characterized by the Pharisees as "publicans and sinners." Tax collectors worked for King Herod and for the Romans. They had great power to search and to take property for the treasury and for themselves. Most Jews hated these people for their cruelty and for their association with the foreign government. The Pharisees rigorously separated themselves from such notable sinners.

Jesus took a much different approach to the situation. Levi probably sat near the boat docks at Capernaum to collect taxes on both imports and exports. He heard Jesus preaching around the shore and responded to Jesus' invitation. Levi's dinner gave Jesus an opportunity to preach to a group of people often excluded from the synagogue and from mainstream Jewish society. Christ explained to the Pharisees that the tax collectors were sick and needed a doctor, which was a common proverb about compassion at the time. Notice that Jesus implied that He was the doctor. Also, He told them plainly that His mission was to call "sinners to repentance." The Pharisees' desire for outward piety through total separation from sinners failed to meet God's desire to reach those sinful men.

The next scene (Mark 2:18-22) involves Christ, the disciples of John the Baptist, and the Pharisees in a conversation about fasting. Moses' law required fasting on the great Day of Atonement, which occurred one day each year. Through the years, the Jews began to fast more often as a means to draw closer to God. The Pharisees fasted twice per week according to Luke 18:12.

It is important to note that Jesus did not condemn the practice, but encouraged fasting privately and not as a public demonstration. Jesus used a familiar wedding custom to tell them that His disciples would fast at a later date. For now, they would not fast because He was still with them. He also used two parable-like comparisons to announce that He was setting aside traditional practices in favor of something new. The man-made constraints of their religion could not hold the forthcoming power and victory of a relationship with God through Christ.

Strict Sabbath observances also characterized the Pharisees' religion. Mark tells us that the Pharisees watched Jesus and the disciples walking through a grain field. The disciples picked some of the grain, removed the chaff, and then ate. The Pharisees accused Jesus of not controlling His disciples by exclaiming, "Behold, why do they on the Sabbath day that which is not lawful" (Mark 2:23-28). Old Testament law did prohibit work on the Sabbath in order to give people physical rest and the time for worship. It allowed acts of kindness and compassion to meet human needs. Jesus also argued in Luke 14:5 that men rescued their animals that had fallen into pits on the Sabbath out of a sense of compassion.

The Sabbath day was God's gift to man and was not to be a tool for oppression. The "law" referred to by the Pharisees was their own oral tradition created by rabbis through the years. They identified thirty-nine types of work and many more subtypes that were prohibited on the Sabbath. Simple tasks were often equated with work. Pulling out a hair was the equivalent of shearing sheep. Picking a few heads of grain corresponded to reaping a field. Jesus reminded them of a time when King David ate some bread that was only for the priests. His actions broke the letter of the law, but upheld the spirit of the law, which is compassion for the needs of men. Jesus also reminded the Pharisees that the Sabbath was created for man's benefit, and that He controlled the specific manner of Sabbath observances. Again, Jesus asserted His deity and authority while laying aside the man-made religion of the Pharisees.

Mark now turns our attention to a synagogue service in Capernaum (Mark 3:1-6). The Pharisees watched Christ to entangle Him in a violation of their teachings. Healing was strictly prohibited on the Sabbath according to their tradition. A man with a withered, or useless, hand was present. An ancient historical reference indicates that he was a stonemason or a plasterer. If the reference is accurate, the man was in a desperate condition because he could not work in his profession. Jesus gave the Pharisees an opportunity to acknowledge the true meaning of the Sabbath. When they refused to answer, Jesus healed the man by simply speaking to him. They heard the teaching of Christ and witnessed His power and compassion. Instead of rejoicing with the healed man and trying to learn more of Christ, they conspired with the Herodians to kill Him. Edmond Hiebert correctly observes that the Pharisees "regarded it a terrible crime for Jesus to heal on the Sabbath, but they had no qualms about plotting murder on the Sabbath!" (Hiebert, 87).

Conspiracy Against Christ
Mark 3:7–14:42

The curiosity of the local religious leaders now extended to the religious establishment in Jerusalem. In the last chapter, we studied the evil accusation of the Jerusalem scribes as recorded in Mark 3:22-30. Christ continued His ministry in spite of the criticism. In fact, more people seemed to follow Christ after that incident. The hostility of the scribes and Pharisees also increased. They looked for ways to trap and to condemn Jesus.

We will not have time to examine each confrontation between Jesus and the religious leaders. You may study them on your own or as a class exercise. We will watch as Christ defends Himself against foolish accusations and challenges the entrenched practices of the day. Jesus wanted to clearly distinguish Himself from the traditions and to warn everyone, including the scribes and Pharisees, about the danger of clinging to a defective religion. In every case, the defect centered on a failure either to know or to apply the Word of God properly. Once again, each scene shows us the glory of knowing Christ personally.

In Mark 7, another group of scribes and Pharisees came from Jerusalem to watch Jesus and to try to discredit His ministry. They saw some of the disciples eating a meal without going through the elaborate hand-washing ceremonies. Mark devotes two verses to explaining the custom for the benefit of non-Jewish readers. About thirty chapters of the Talmud discuss all the procedures and practices for washing both hands and pots. The process of purification was one of the central themes of the Pharisees' religion. According to their own words, the ritual came from the "tradition of the elders" and not from the law of Moses (Mark 7:5). The word *tradition* occurs five times in this chapter. We can therefore conclude that Jesus' words constitute His formal evaluation of the Jewish customs.

Notice that He first turned their attention to the prophet Isaiah. God used Isaiah to condemn outward religion that never reaches the heart. The source of this defective religion is the replacement of God's Word with man's traditions. Jesus then recounted to them their practice of dishonoring parents. The Pharisees would vow to give all their money to the temple. If elderly parents needed financial assistance, the Pharisee would refuse to give it to them based on the fact that it was devoted to God. The result was an impoverished parent and the breaking of the fifth commandment (Exod. 20:12). Tradition supplanted God's very clear precept of honoring parents.

Jesus then called the multitude together and exposed the theological fallacy practiced by the religious leadership. Traditional Jewish theology taught that man is good, and that he may choose good or evil based on external influences. Conforming to outward standards of conduct pointed to inward purity. Jesus told the multitude—and later the disciples—that man is only defiled by what

TEXT

TOOLS

Commentaries: Tools for Understanding

Bible scholars often write books to help Christians understand the text and application of the Scriptures. When studying the Bible, you should always read the text several times and record your thoughts on paper. Use a dictionary to look up unfamiliar words. Try to find the main teaching of the passage. Then, use a conservative commentary to supply details about the culture, language, and interpretation of the verses.

One very good commentary on Mark is Edmond Hiebert's *The Gospel of Mark,* published by BJU Press. The following selection deals with Jesus' warning to the disciples about the teachings of the Pharisees in Mark 8:15.

THE
GOSPEL
OF
MARK

An Expositional Commentary

D. Edmond Hiebert

"Take heed . . . beware of"—the utterance of a double caution. Both verbs are present imperatives, stressing attitudes that ought to continue. The first verb calls for mental alertness, while the second demands that they look attentively at the object called to their attention in order to avoid the danger it presents.

"The leaven of the Pharisees and of the leaven of Herod"—the repeated definite noun, *the leaven,* views the two leavens as distinct yet closely related as a common moral danger because both were allied against Christ. Since leaven was strictly forbidden with certain offerings (Lev. 2:11) and had to be removed during the Passover, it readily became a figure of evil or corruption. This was the meaning given it in rabbinical teaching and seems to be its uniform meaning in the New Testament. As producing a process of fermentation, leaven or yeast pictures a pervasive corrupting tendency that works invisibly. Christ's warning was thus "a pithy one-word parable for unseen pervasive influence." Mark did not give us an interpretation of Christ's meaning, but Matthew (16:12) noted that His reference was to "the teaching" of those warned against. Clearly Christ was thinking of the penetrating and corrupting influence of the teachings of His opponents. His warning against the leaven of the Pharisees is to be understood in the light of what had just occurred [Mark 8:11-13]. Their perverted views concerning moral goodness and moral evil (cf. 7:1-23) left them morally blind and unable to discern the mission and character of the Messiah (Hiebert, 226).

comes out of him. External influences do not defile. The sinful operation of man's heart defiles. Man's problem is not failing to wash hands and pots. It is internal wickedness that only Christ cures through the forgiveness of sins and the beginning of an entirely new life. Many people probably did not understand the magnitude of Christ's words. New life comes not from external ritual, but from embracing the Son of God.

Christ entered the temple near the time of the crucifixion and removed those who used the temple grounds as a marketplace (Mark 11:15-18). The high priest did not allow the use of foreign coins bearing the image of Caesar for the purchase of items needed in worship. Jews from all over the world arrived in Jerusalem to sacrifice and to worship. These travelers required animals and provisions. The priest's family gladly exchanged their Roman coins for temple coins and then sold sacrificial animals at inflated prices. Jesus saw those in the religious establishment using their positions to make money and to exploit faithful Jews. His righteous actions infuriated the scribes and priests.

When Jesus returned to the temple a short time after His expulsion of the money exchangers and merchants, the religious leaders asked Him about the source of His authority. Jesus turned the question back to their rejection of John the Baptist's preaching. Mark 12 then records the final public debate between Christ and the religious leaders. Jesus began by telling the people gathered at the temple a parable about wicked tenant farmers rejecting the owner's messengers and his expectations for fruit. The language reflects a similar story in Isaiah 5 that would have been familiar to the learned scribes. Notice that Jesus implied that He was the son of the owner, a reference to His deity. He also quoted from Psalm 118:22, 23 to tell them that God Himself will overrule the scribes and Pharisees' rejection of the Messiah. The very people that should have been the first to recognize and embrace the Messiah seemed utterly blinded by their religion and greed.

Next, the leaders sent a delegation of Pharisees and Herodians to Jesus to entrap Him in one of the most difficult questions of the time for the Jews. The Roman government imposed heavy taxes on all conquered provinces. The Jews believed that paying the tax was equivalent to accepting Caesar's rule over the sacred land. Failure to pay might provoke military action by the Roman legion. Perhaps they believed that the Romans might take Jesus away if He advocated not paying. If He agreed to pay the tax, then the Pharisees would accuse Him of collusion with the enemy. Jesus looked at a coin and said, "Render to Caesar the things that are Caesar's, and to God the things that are God's" (Mark 12:17). Duties to God and duties to government do not conflict in the issue of tax payments.

The Sadducees then asked Jesus a theoretical question about eternity and the resurrection from the dead (Mark 12:18-27). This group did not believe in the resurrection, and therefore asked the question to entangle Jesus in heresy in order to condemn Him. It's possible that the Sadducees used the same story to frustrate the Pharisees.

Jesus directly rebuked them for being ignorant of the Old Testament Scriptures. He pointed out that heaven is not like earth. Marriage does not exist in eternity; therefore the question is not

Herod's Temple

Jerusalem was the center of national pride and worship for Jews around the world. Herod the Great decided that building a magnificent temple in the city would ensure the loyalty of his divided subjects and would establish his kingdom. The project began in 20 B.C. and was not completed until A.D. 64. Priests, trained by Herod, performed most of the work. Josephus wrote that the white marble and gold structures glistened in the sun and could be seen for miles. As the hub of Jewish religion, the temple contained the furniture, rooms, and equipment for the ritual sacrifices. The New Testament contains many references to Herod's temple. It was destroyed by the Romans in A.D. 70—only six years after its completion.

relevant. Jesus also gave them a lesson in explaining the books of Moses that they claimed to believe. God's statement to Moses at the burning bush implies that Abraham, Isaac, and Jacob lived at that very moment. The book of Genesis records the death of all three. The only reasonable conclusion is that God had raised them from the dead. Every detail of this doctrine may not be clear, but the Sadducees had no excuse for missing the point of the Scriptures.

Finally, a scribe came to Jesus and presented Him with another vexing question (Mark 12:28-34). Jews often debated which commandment was the greatest. Jesus' answer combined two positive aspects of Old Testament religion. The first comes from Deuteronomy 6:4, 5, which states the uniqueness of God's person and man's duty to love Him. He then quoted a more obscure passage from Leviticus 19:18 that summarizes the duties of one man to other men. Note that love is the primary requirement in both situations. The scribe commended Jesus for His wise answer and affirmed that loving God supersedes all sacrifice and ritual. Not every religious leader in Israel was blind to the true intent of the Scriptures.

Jesus had started this debate by asking the religious leaders about John the Baptist's ministry. He ended it by asking about the proper interpretation of Psalm 110, which was universally accepted by the Jews as pointing to the Messiah (Mark 12:35-40). The scribes preached that Messiah would be a direct descendant of King David. In earthly relationships, fathers exercise authority over children. The scribes therefore believed that Messiah would submit to David as a son submitted to a father. Jesus quoted Psalm 110:1, in which David calls Messiah by the title "my Lord."

In Jewish thought, a father would never call a child "my Lord." The leaders failed to understand that Messiah was more than a physical descendant of David. Messiah was both God and man through the miracle of the incarnation. Jesus wanted to show them the weakness of their interpretations and teachings. The common man in the temple probably rejoiced that Jesus had confounded the scribes and Pharisees. Jesus then sternly warned the people to beware of the blatant hypocrisy of the religious leadership. In contrast, He noted the simple godliness of a poor widow contributing to the temple treasury (Mark 12:41-44).

Condemnation of Christ
Mark 14:43–15:47

Jesus knew exactly what the religious establishment planned to do with Him. He also knew that God had planned His death to bring about man's eternal salvation from sin. His task was to obey God and to deliver one last direct witness of the truth to the leaders of Israel. The critical moment came as the leaders brought Jesus to trial before the Sanhedrin in Mark 14:53-65. Jesus did not respond as witnesses presented conflicting evidence of His guilt. Finally, out of a sense of frustration, the high priest asked Jesus directly, "Art thou the Christ, the Son of the Blessed?" The question probably echoed what the high priest had heard about Jesus and does not indicate that the man believed it. Again, he was looking for a way to trap Jesus and to give them an excuse to kill Him. This time, Jesus answered in such a way as to prick their consciences with the truth that they claimed to believe. "I am" could be a direct reference to the Old Testament name of God given to Moses at the burning bush (Exod. 3:14).

The Jews reverenced this name to the point that they would not speak it for fear of defiling God's character in some way. Jesus' response could also be a shortened form of "I am the Christ, the Son of the Blessed." Either way, the message was clear. Jesus confessed His true identity. He likewise alluded to His coming judgment upon their sin by using language similar to that in Daniel 7:13 and Psalm 110:1. Christ's confession should have caused them to stop and consider this person whom they wanted to condemn. But they rushed forward with a sentence of guilt and took Jesus to Pilate for the official death sentence. The Romans did not empower the Jewish council to put anyone to death.

The high priest, acting as the chief political and religious figure in Israel, convened a meeting with the other religious leaders to plan a believable indictment of Christ before the Roman governor (Mark 15:1). Pilate finally accepted the guilty verdict and crucified Jesus. In one last act of cruelty and rejection, the leaders mocked Christ as He hung on the cross (Mark 15:31, 32).

Three days later, the disciples wondered and rejoiced over the fulfillment of Psalm 118:22, 23: "The stone which the builders refused is become the head stone of the corner. This is the Lord's doing; it is marvellous in our eyes." Christ rose from the dead to vindicate His authority and teaching. Even so, the Gospel of Matthew records the scheme of the religious leaders to discredit the Resurrection (Matt. 28:11-15).

The Mocking of Christ, *by Northern follower of Caravaggio, Bob Jones University Collection*

Final Thoughts

The Bible portrays the best and worst of man's nature: the depravity of the wicked religious leaders helps us to better discern the glory of Jesus Christ. Even the very best of men will disappoint you at some time. As you survey religious movements and organizations today, you are very likely to see many characteristics of the scribes and Pharisees. Let those perceptions drive you to a close relationship with the Son of God. Rejecting man's religious traditions in favor of God's clear teaching in the Bible will bring the scorn of many people. The Lord may be opening an opportunity for you to present the truth to them. They rejected Christ and they may reject you. If following Christ means walking contrary to man's religion, then so be it. "That I may know him" must be the goal of our lives.

Review Questions

A. Traditions   F. Pilate
B. Not in NT   G. Tax collector
C. 70   H. Followers of a king
D. Priests   I. Temple builder
E. Disciple   J. Law experts

____1. Scribes   ____6. Governor

____2. Pharisees   ____7. Herod the Great

____3. Herodians   ____8. Publican

____4. Essenes   ____9. Sadducees

____5. Sanhedrin

Essay

10. Why did the scribes and Pharisees consider Jesus to be a threat?

11. Why were the Pharisees upset that Jesus associated with the publicans?

12. What is the "tradition of the elders"?

13. Why did the priest prohibit Roman coins in the temple?

14. How did Jesus summarize the law of Moses in Mark 12?

15. Why did the Jewish leaders condemn Christ at His trial?

Christ and the Disciples—Part I

6

Beth Kent flipped through the pages of her music scrapbook. Beth's mother took pictures at every recital and concert, and also collected the programs and awards. She then assembled the articles onto the pages of a large scrapbook. At first, Beth had thought that her mother's efforts were a waste of time. But now that she was nearly ready to graduate from high school, she enjoyed looking at the pages before a concert. Remembering the years of hard work seemed to help her get ready to play her instrument. Beth was now the principal cellist in the high school orchestra. Mr. Fredrick, the orchestra conductor, depended on her leadership to help the younger musicians play together and stay in tune.

Beth's mother came into the room and sat down beside her. They turned to the beginning of the book where Beth was shown in second grade, just starting to play piano. The tiny quarter-size cello first appeared in fourth grade, the year she started taking lessons. By seventh grade, she had a half-size cello and braces on her teeth. The braces disappeared in tenth grade. By then she also had a full-size cello and several awards for playing excellence.

"What do you notice about every page in the scrapbook from fourth grade until now?" her mom asked.

Beth quickly turned through a dozen or more pages and the answer seemed obvious.

"Mom, Mrs. Matthews is everywhere! She is either teaching me, sitting in the front row of the audience during a concert, or standing next to me during an award presentation."

Mrs. Kent said, "Do you remember when she informed us that you had little chance for success with the cello? You started practicing for forty-five minutes every day just to prove her wrong!"

"I well remember that day. I think she was just trying to get me going! After nine years of weekly lessons with her, the thing that I appreciate the most is that Mrs. Matthews can play cello better than anyone else I know. She explains techniques and music theory, but then she shows me how to do it. Playing with her is the very best part of learning cello."

Her mother interrupted her and said, "Your dad and I appreciate Mrs. Matthews's determination to make you a good cello player. But, if we don't leave soon, you will be late for the concert, and all of us will be in trouble!"

The Kents arrived in plenty of time for the performance. Parents, classmates, teachers, and friends enjoyed every minute of the hour-long concert. And of course, Mrs. Matthews sat right in the front row.

Once, after hearing a talented musician, I tried to teach myself how to play the piano. After a few hours, I could tap out one or two lines of a song, but I soon gave up. Piano was a lot of work and required more dedication than I was willing to put into it by myself. Perhaps a teacher could have guided me about timing and hand techniques. Being responsible to a teacher could have motivated me to keep trying and to make steady progress. Beth's skill at the cello was due in part to her relationship with her teacher.

Many young Christians approach their relationship to Christ as I approached the piano. We want the benefits, but are unwilling to learn from the Teacher. Being a disciple of Christ does place some demands upon us. Jesus constantly teaches us lessons, and we must respond accordingly. In this chapter, we will examine Christ's program for developing His followers. By carefully learning from our master teacher and then following His example, my life as a believer will grow and flourish. I may never be able to play the piano or the cello due to my lack of talent and skill. But I can follow Christ. More importantly, He can transform my life into something truly productive for the kingdom of God.

The Call to Discipleship
Mark 1:16-20; 3:13-19

The Gospel of John records Jesus' first personal contact with some of the disciples (John 1:35-51). John the Baptist openly identified Jesus as the Lamb of God and then encouraged his disciples to follow Jesus. These men recognized Jesus as a Rabbi or teacher (John 1:38), as the Messiah (John 1:41), and as the Son of God and King of Israel (John 1:49). We may assume that Christ's public teachings and private conversations helped them to understand His person. The text does not indicate that they stayed with Him all the time. As Jesus preached around Galilee and Jordan, they gladly listened and believed.

Mark's first mention of the disciples, in Mark 1:16-20, actually occurred in the second year of Jesus' public ministry. Nearly a year later—after Herod had imprisoned John the Baptist—Jesus once again ministered in Galilee. This is when He called two sets of brothers to follow Him full-time. Notice that Jesus used language that the fishermen would readily understand. Their fathers had taught them the fishing business; now Jesus wanted to teach them how to fish for men. *Come ye after me* simply means to follow. Teachers in ancient times would walk from one place to the next while students walked behind or beside them. Students would listen and ask questions along the way. Simon, Andrew, James, and John quickly left their fishing business to learn the much greater business of reaching men.

Some months later, the Jewish religious leadership began to oppose Christ's ministry and teaching. By that time, large crowds followed Jesus because they recognized His great power and authority. Jesus personally selected twelve men for two important purposes. Mark 3:14 says that these men "should be with him," which indicates a special closeness to and fellowship with the Teacher. The same verse also tells us that He would "send them forth to preach." We get the English word *apostle* from the Greek word translated "send forth." These were Jesus' disciples and apostles. He would first teach them about God's kingdom, and then send them out to preach the gospel.

Let's briefly examine some facts about these twelve men. All, except for perhaps Judas Iscariot, were from Galilee and not from the center of Jewish religion in Jerusalem. None were scribes, priests, or Pharisees. Matthew worked for the government as a tax collector. Simon the Canaanite or Zealot opposed the government through sabotage and subversion. James and John, nicknamed by Jesus as the sons of thunder, were probably emotional and restless. Logically, we might expect Jesus to choose high-class religious leaders as His closest associates for spreading God's Word to Israel. Instead, He selected lowly men who responded to His Word. They left jobs, businesses, families, and other personal interests to follow the Son of God and to seek the souls of men.

Calming the Sea
Mark 4:35-41

Christ's training of the disciples now took a new direction. They had just completed a day of public instruction and private lessons about the kingdom of God. Jesus was tired and so were the disciples. To escape the multitudes and to get some rest, He directed them to take a boat to the other side of the lake. As the fishermen sailed across the water, Jesus slept on a pillow in the back of the ship. Suddenly a great storm of wind and waves came upon them.

The Sea of Galilee is actually over six hundred feet below sea level and is surrounded by many mountains. The warm waters attract violent weather even today. High winds kicked up waves that filled the boat with water. Some of the disciples probably bailed water out of the boat. Others tried to steady the sail or held on to the side to keep from being thrown overboard. "Carest thou not that we perish?" shows us that the fishermen's skill and experience on the water was no match for the storm. The words seem to rebuke Jesus for sleeping and for showing little concern for their dire condition.

Jesus was now ready to teach them an important lesson about Himself. As the Son of God, the waves were not a threat to Him. He simply got up from the pillow and calmed the storm by His word. The howling wind stopped immediately when Jesus commanded *Peace,* which means "be quiet" or "be silent." *Be still* comes from a word that means "to be muzzled." Jesus then rebuked the disciples for their lack of faith, which had turned to fearfulness. He fully expected them to recognize His deity. Had He not cast out demons and healed many of the sick? The disciples now feared Jesus more than they feared the storm. A true disciple of Christ will recognize that Jesus is God and will rest in His concern for him.

Ministering in the Villages
Mark 6:7-13

The people of Nazareth did not accept the teachings of Christ. He understood that opposition to His work would increase as time passed. He also knew that the disciples needed to learn some important lessons about the nature of the ministry. Sending the disciples to the villages would certainly spread the news of salvation to more people, and it would also give the twelve some very valuable experiences. They listened to Jesus' teaching, saw His great compassion, and experienced His power over the sea. Now they must learn by doing the work that Jesus did. But this time, the disciples would do it without Jesus' presence.

Notice that he sent them out in teams of two. Old Testament law required two witnesses to an event. A single person could make up a wild story or bring a false accusation against another. The Israelites were to dismiss the claims of a single source. Jesus

wanted the disciples to have credibility, and so He wisely sent them two by two. Likewise, Jesus gave them authority over unclean spirits so that people would listen more attentively to their preaching.

He gave them very strict instructions about physical provisions along the way. They could take the shoes, clothing, and the walking stick of a common poor traveler, and nothing else. Jesus wanted to teach them to depend upon God for their daily provisions. He also wanted them to avoid

The Fish Symbol

Early Christians used the fish as a symbol of their faith. When meeting a stranger, a believer would draw one arc of the symbol on the ground. If the other person drew the other arc, they both knew that they shared a love for Christ. They could then openly share their faith without fear of persecution.

The Greek word for fish, *ichthus*, forms an acronym for Jesus Christ, God the Son, Savior. From the very beginning of church history, believers recognized Jesus' association with fish and fishing. Read the following passages and write a simple newspaper headline about Christ's connection with the fishing industry.

Mark 1:16-20 _____

Luke 5:3-11 _____

Matthew 13:47-49 _____

_____

Mark 6:30-44 _____

_____

Mark 8:1-9 _____

_____

John 21:1-14 _____

_____

any association with heathen religious practices. Some groups would travel the roads to collect money for their temples and places of worship.

Observe also the importance that Jesus placed on their work. The disciples were to travel to the villages and preach the Word of God. He fully expected the people to receive them and to show them customary Jewish hospitality. Those places that rejected the words of the disciples subjected themselves to God's judgment. God destroyed Sodom and Gomorrah for their vile sexual practices.

Ministering to Others

A vital part of growing in your relationship to Christ is learning how to tell others about the Savior. Fear of rejection or of not knowing what to say often stops believers from obeying the Lord in this matter.

The disciples spoke about the kingdom of God and about repenting of sin. You can do the same in many different ways. Giving out gospel tracts is a simple means of witnessing. You can tell someone about your personal testimony of faith in Christ or start a general conversation with someone and then turn the focus to spiritual issues. You might say, "I'm a Christian and if you will give me a few minutes, I would like to tell you about the Lord." Then share verses from the Bible that explain the plan of salvation. Many people use the following verses called the Romans Road to witness for Christ.

Romans 3:23—All are sinful.

Romans 6:23—The penalty for sin is death.

Romans 14:12—God will judge all men.

Romans 5:8—Christ died in our place.

Romans 10:9, 13—People must believe in Christ.

Even today, these cities are a symbol of wickedness and of God's condemnation of sin. Jesus told the disciples that rejection of their preaching was a greater sin than the sin of Sodom and Gomorrah. Men rejected Jesus and they would also reject the disciples.

Christ wanted them to experience every aspect of the work, including its success. Notice in Mark 6:12, 13 that they preached the same message as Christ, and likewise cast out demons and healed the sick. Verse 30 records the return and the report of the disciples. You can almost hear the excited enthusiasm as they "told him **all** things, both what they had done, and what they had taught [emphasis added]."

Cooperating in the Ministry I
Mark 6:30-44

The story of the feeding of the five thousand is very familiar to most of us. But have you ever considered Christ's purpose for this event? Jesus quietly revealed His power as God while allowing the disciples to cooperate in the work and ministry to the masses. We will see again that discipleship is recognizing Christ's person and then following His teaching and direction for our lives.

After the disciples reported to Jesus about their work, He knew that they needed rest. They tried to travel privately by boat to the other side of Galilee, but the multitudes saw them. Some ran around the lake to the other side and met Jesus when the boat arrived. Christ saw their needs and desire for instruction, and He began to teach them.

We can assume that He was probably as tired as the others. Christ's compassion toward human adversity motivated Him to continue. The disciples seem to rebuke Jesus for the long teaching session when they suggested that He send the people away to buy food. His response, "Give ye them to eat," must have startled the disciples. They reasoned that the equivalent of eight months of a laborer's salary would be needed to buy enough bread for all the people. The prospects seemed impossible. By now, we tend to expect the disciples to catch on to the fact that Jesus, as God, was capable of meeting this need. Christ told the twelve to find out how much food was present. The report came back that they had five small loaves of barley bread and two small salted fish, which was about the size of a boy's lunch.

Christ commanded the crowd to sit down in groups of fifty and one hundred so all might be served in an orderly fashion. He then prayed a blessing, broke the bread and fish, and gave them to the disciples for distribution. Right before the disciples' eyes, Jesus multiplied a meager lunch to feed a multitude. Most of the crowd probably did not realize what Jesus was doing. The meal was very simple, but it filled them. They were glad for the food and for the teaching. Christ cared for both the physical and spiritual needs of the people. The disciples saw Christ's compassion and His power. He allowed them to participate in the work as they obeyed His directions. The union between the divine Christ and obedient disciples would become the pattern for all spiritual victories.

Teachings on the Sea
Mark 6:45-54

Jesus' next two lessons for the twelve are similar to previous ones. Some critics of the Bible contend that the same events are recorded twice due to an editorial error. These people fail to understand the nature of the Bible's inspiration and the depravity of the human heart. Christ repeated the teachings because the disciples failed to understand their true significance the first time. You and I likewise seldom comprehend spiritual lessons the first time. Mark adds a comment to the end of this section, which summarizes the real issue. "For they considered not the miracle of the loaves: for their heart was hardened" (Mark 6:52). The Lord expects us to see His working and instruction through His Word and the circumstances of our lives. Followers of Christ often fail their Master. We can be thankful that He will try again to teach us those lessons that elude our understanding. The Lord is merciful to us in our weakness.

Immediately after feeding the masses, Jesus compelled the disciples to leave for the other side of the lake by boat. The word *constrained* indicates that He had to persuade them to leave. Something seems to have aroused the disciples or the crowd. Perhaps the people wanted Jesus to start a revolution against the Romans. Perhaps they just wanted to be fed again. Christ dismissed the people and went to a mountain to pray. Verse 47 signifies that the time was early evening or around 6 P.M. He could clearly see the disciples rowing the boat into a mighty wind toward the other side. By the fourth watch of the night or about 3 A.M., Jesus walked on the water going to the other side. Mark

George Mueller: Faith in God's Provision PRINCIPLES APPLIED

George Mueller (1805-1898) lived a very wicked life while studying for the ministry in Eastern Europe. At a prayer meeting, he repented and believed in Christ. His life changed radically. In time the Lord led him to Bristol, England, to pastor a church and eventually to start numerous ministries for the poor, including several orphanages. Mueller's great faith in God's provision for the physical needs of His people continues to encourage believers today. Mueller believed in asking God alone to provide for the children. He would not appeal to people for money or other necessities. Biographies of Mueller abound with God's answers to his prayers. The following excerpt is from A. T. Pierson, Mueller's son-in-law. In this situation, all funds were depleted and they could look only to God for help. Notice the strong faith of the house parent.

"A gentleman and some ladies visiting the orphan house saw the large number of little ones to be cared for. One of the ladies said to the matron of the Boys' House: 'Of course you cannot carry on these institutions without a good stock of funds'; and the gentleman added, 'Have you a good stock?' The quiet answer was, 'Our funds are deposited in a bank which cannot break.' The reply drew tears from the eyes of the lady, and a gift of five pounds from the pocket of the gentleman—a donation most opportune, as there was not one penny then in hand."

Have you learned the lesson that God can supply for your needs? We should be like David when he cried, "The Lord is my shepherd, I shall not want" (Psalm 23:1).

tells us that Christ "would have passed by them" (Mark 6:48). The disciples' wearisome trial is nothing for the Son of God. The sight of Christ on the water caused the disciples to stop fearing the elements. They now feared Christ. His words of comfort to them again revealed His identity. *It is I* is the Greek expression of the Hebrew name of God revealed to Moses in Exodus 3. When Jesus got into the boat, the wind ceased and the twelve were astonished. The disciples' safety rested in the deity of Christ. True discipleship focuses on the person and work of God's Son.

Cooperating in the Ministry II
Mark 8:1-9

The feeding of the four thousand is another very familiar story to us. Differences from the feeding of the five thousand include the number of people present, the amount of food at the beginning and at the end, and the type of vessel used to store the gathered fragments. In Mark 6, the disciples used small lunch pouches, which were generally carried around the waist. This time, they used larger baskets that may have stored fish.

Jesus makes His two purposes for this event very clear to us. The multitude had been listening to Him teach for three days without the opportunity to obtain food. Some of the people had probably brought provisions with them, but even their supply was now exhausted. Jesus simply wanted to show compassion for their physical needs. Most of us would not endure three days of spiritual instruction without focusing on food.

Observe Jesus' second purpose as He presents the problem to the disciples. He expects them to believe that He is able to provide the food. Just a few months before, they had seen Him feed an even larger crowd. Their answer in Mark 8:4 shows that they still looked to human wisdom as a means of meeting men's needs. The twelve stood in the presence of God's Son, but did not comprehend His ability to solve the problem. Jesus wanted to show them His power once again that they might recognize Him. He took the food, blessed it, broke it, and gave it to the disciples for distribution to the people. This time, they gathered seven large baskets of leftovers. Jesus probably used the larger baskets and larger quantity of fragments as a visual lesson for the disciples. Who else but God could multiply a small lunch into such abundance?

A very short time later (Mark 8:10-21), the Pharisees asked Jesus for a sign of His authority and He refused to give one to them. He then got into a boat with the disciples and warned them about the doctrine of the religious leaders. The warning came in the form of a figure of speech about leaven, which symbolized sin. The disciples thought that Jesus was concerned about their lack of bread on the boat. He chastised them for not learning that He could supply all the bread they needed. Christ's main concern was spiritual. The disciples saw only the physical. Even after a second lesson, the disciples failed to understand the person and power of Christ.

Training for Discipleship
Mark 8:27–9:1

Jesus now deliberately led the disciples away from the crowds around Galilee toward Caesarea Philippi. He needed a quieter place to privately teach the twelve some very important concepts about Himself and about life. As they walked along, He asked them who other people thought He might be. The group had certainly heard chatter about Him in the marketplaces and synagogues. Their answers revealed that the Jews regarded Jesus as a great man. Some superstitiously thought that He was John the Baptist raised from the dead.

Jesus then focused the disciples' attention on the real issue by asking what they thought. Peter answered correctly by proclaiming that Jesus was the Christ or the Messiah. All the months of

THOU ART THE CHRIST

teaching, observation, and work finally came to fruition. But their concept of the Messiah was flawed. Like most Jews, they expected a political kingdom that would restore national sovereignty to Israel. Jesus revealed to them that He would die at the hands of the religious leadership in Jerusalem. Three days later, He would rise from the dead.

Peter decided to correct the Lord's thinking by talking to Him away from the others. Jesus' words probably never left Peter's mind. "Get thee behind me, Satan: for thou savourest not the things that be of God, but the things that be of men" (Mark 8:33). Jesus corrected Peter's thinking. God's will was for Jesus to die in the place of sinners. Christ would then secure eternal life for His people. The political kingdom would come much later. Jesus' words to Peter were very strong. Peter needed to understand the entire truth about the person of Christ, and so must all of His disciples. We may not fully comprehend the depths of Christ's person and work, but we must accept them as truth.

Jesus then began to instruct them about the true nature of discipleship. Christ expounds three requirements; they teach us that a true disciple will follow the steps of His master. First, disciples must deny themselves. At the very heart of sin is the desire to put self first. Adam and Eve acted out of self-interest when they ate the fruit in Eden. Satan convinced Eve that God withheld something good from them and that they could gain it back by disobedience to God's clear command. Jesus certainly denied Himself by coming to earth to die for sinners.

Second, a disciple must take up the cross. The Jews were very familiar with the cross as a form of execution and torture. The Romans did everything possible to make shameful examples of those who defied their law. Jesus would suffer on a cross for doing the will of God. Disciples must likewise understand that the world is antagonistic toward God. Those who follow Christ must willingly accept the reproach of the world.

Third, the disciple of Christ must follow Christ. The verb *follow* is in the present tense indicating that the action is continuous. Believers do the things that Jesus did.

The cost of discipleship is very high. Logically, we may wonder why anyone would want to meet Christ's conditions for following Him. Jesus anticipated the question and proceeded to give several answers which focus on eternal values.

First, in Mark 8:35, Jesus clearly states that those who act to save their current lives will actually lose their lives. The opposite is also true. Those who lose their lives will gain them. Christ willingly lost His life for our sakes and then gained it back at His Resurrection. Believers can expect to do the same.

Second, nothing compares to the value of the soul. Man cannot buy his life with all the goods in the world. Therefore, losing your life to gain eternal life is a great bargain.

Third, a day of great judgment is coming. A person's relationship to Christ and to the world will be the basis of judgment. Those who deny Christ to gain favor with the world will suffer great loss.

Some Final Thoughts

Jesus taught the disciples many lessons. Keep in mind that the twelve were almost always present as Christ healed the sick, cast out demons, preached to the crowds, and rebuked the religious leaders. He also sent them out to work alone. They often failed to understand His lessons. We might be tempted to give them a poor grade for substandard performance. Being a disciple of Christ means that we have a close and energetic relationship with Him. What lessons is Jesus teaching you today? Do you increasingly recognize Him as God? Would He give you a passing grade as a disciple?

Review Questions

_____ 1. Jesus called James and John to leave their fishing business in the first year of His ministry.

_____ 2. *Apostle* means "to follow."

_____ 3. The Sea of Galilee is six hundred feet above sea level.

_____ 4. The Old Testament required four witnesses to verify the truthfulness of a testimony or claim.

_____ 5. Gomorrah is a symbol of wickedness.

_____ 6. The fourth watch of the night started at 10 p.m.

_____ 7. The disciples gathered seven baskets of leftovers at the feeding of the four thousand.

_____ 8. Jesus stopped teaching the disciples when they recognized Him as God.

_____ 9. Jesus taught the disciples that Messiah would die in Galilee.

_____ 10. A man's soul is worth more than all the money in the world.

11. Compare or contrast how Jesus' death paralleled His requirements for being a disciple.

12. Why did Jesus not choose His disciples from the religious leadership in Jerusalem?

13. What did Jesus do to help the disciples' credibility as they ministered in the villages in Mark 6:7-13?

14. Why did Jesus walk on the water in Mark 6:45-54?

15. How can a person lose his life by saving it?

Christ and the Disciples—Part II

7

Ten guys and girls sat in the new ice cream parlor near the school. Third quarter exams were now completed, and the teachers planned to post grades in two days. Normally, the "lunch crew," as they called themselves, would celebrate the end of exams by getting together for a short party. The tradition included a strict rule about not discussing tests and projects. But this time, the discussion centered on Mr. Franklin's long essay questions in English literature. Everybody's answers seemed to be different. Several worried out loud about the potential effect the test might have on the report cards. The "lunch crew" had been together in school since third grade and could well empathize with each other's situations.

Jerry spoke up, "It seems to me that we are straying from our tradition of trying to forget about exams. Let's all get ice cream cones this time and talk about anything other than Milton and Shakespeare."

The server came and patiently took each order. Anna was the last one to decide which flavor she wanted.

Anna finally said, "I will take cherry chocolate chip in a cone. Could you please include a spoon with mine?"

Cindy asked, "Who ever heard of someone eating an ice cream cone with a spoon? I thought cones were for licking!"

Everyone, including Anna, just laughed. The conversation quickly returned to the school year and to graduation. Soon, the servers returned with ten huge ice cream cones and Anna's spoon.

After three or four satisfying licks on the ice cream cones, almost everyone noticed Anna's technique. She carefully dug through the vanilla ice cream with the spoon to extract the cherries and chocolate chips, which she delightedly ate. Every minute or two, she would lick the vanilla to find more cherries.

Anna noticed the attention and slyly said, "Yes, I'm different! Mr. Franklin said in English class that a good way to analyze an author is to find one or two key themes and to look for them in the literature. It worked well in class. I thought I would try it with ice cream. The key themes today are cherries and chocolate chips! My essay thesis will be 'Frozen cherries are delicious'!"

Larry replied, "The cold ice cream probably got into the cherries to make them taste better, but they're not frozen anymore. Just look at the puddle of vanilla on the table and on your hand."

Anna quickly abandoned her spoon and began eating in earnest.

Our "ice cream cone" is our study of Mark's Gospel. The cherries are Christ's relationships with various groups of people. His power and compassion should give us a great foundation for living in this world. Much of Jesus' work focused on training the twelve disciples. In the last chapter, we saw Him patiently revealing His deity to them. Knowledge always brings responsibility. The disciples knew that Jesus was the Messiah; now they must learn to follow Him. In this chapter we will see Jesus patiently explaining to the twelve what it means to be a follower or a disciple. He will also show them through His example. At times, we might consider Christ's requirements to be difficult. The disciples constantly saw Jesus' power. They knew that He was God. When we focus on Christ's person and power as God, the requirements for discipleship will be delightful. Anna used a spoon to dig cherries and chocolate chips out of her vanilla ice cream. We will use our Bible study skills to "dig out" teachings on Christ's deity and our discipleship from the last months of Jesus' time on earth.

The Transfiguration
Mark 9:1-13

Peter's great confession about Jesus' being the Messiah was simply the introduction to several teachings that must have startled the disciples. Jesus told them that He would die. If they wanted to be His disciples, they must follow the same path of self-denial. Christ rose from the dead, and similarly the disciples would also enjoy the benefits of a new life. The Jews' concept of the Messiah was much different. They looked for a political and military leader.

Jesus took Peter, James, and John to an isolated mountain to teach them about His deity and the truthfulness of His teachings. Mark 9:2 tells us that Jesus was "transfigured" or "metamorphosed." Most will recognize the word from a study of biology. It means to change into another form, just as a caterpillar changes into a butterfly. Mark emphasizes that this change was not of human origin. No man could have made Jesus' shining clothing. Peter, James, and John saw Jesus in His glorified body. He was God and He was human. They also saw Moses and Elijah talking to Jesus. Moses represented the law while Elijah represented the prophets. Both wrote about Christ. Luke's Gospel tells us that they spoke about Jesus' death.

Out of fear, Peter asked Jesus if he could build three tents, presumably for prolonging the experience. God the Father then spoke to the group from a cloud, "This is my beloved Son: hear him." God identified Jesus as His Son and also validated the lessons that Christ taught the disciples. Remember that the Old Testament required two or three witnesses to confirm the truthfulness of a claim. Peter, James, and John had now heard from three great witnesses that Jesus was God and that He would die for sinners.

As the four departed from the mountain, Jesus told them not to tell anyone about the experience until He was risen from the dead. They failed to understand the Resurrection, but feared to ask Him about it. Rather, they asked about a less important issue regarding the scribes' teaching on Elijah. They believed that

Elijah would reappear before the coming of Messiah. Jesus told them that Elijah had already appeared. He referred to the ministry of John the Baptist, which the religious leaders rejected. More importantly, Jesus focused their attention back on His death and suffering. The second part of Mark 9:12 should be punctuated as a question. Jesus was trying to direct their minds away from secondary issues so that they might concentrate on His death.

Christ Teaches About His Death
Mark 9:30-32; 10:32-34

On at least two occasions in the weeks prior to His death, Jesus taught the disciples about His death. The length of the recorded teaching probably does not reflect the actual time Jesus spent on the subject. *Taught* in Mark 9:31 is in the imperfect tense, indicating that the action was continuous or not complete. The group walked from around Caesarea Philippi to Capernaum, a trip of about forty miles, which would take at least two days. Jesus had ample opportunity to speak to the twelve on the road or during breaks for meals. They could then think about His words as they walked.

Notice the specifics of Jesus' teaching. He would be delivered into the hands of men. *Deliver* is a passive form meaning that someone else would deliver Jesus. The subject is not definite. It may be that Jesus referred to the betrayal of Judas. More likely, He

The Christ of Derision, *by Philippe de Champaigne, Bob Jones University Collection*

116

Bible Study Techniques

A great way to study the Bible is to write a one-sentence summary about the main teaching of a chapter or paragraph. This method can be difficult at first, but it gets easier with practice. Successful athletes work hard at perfecting their skills over time. Christians should do the same. Use the following steps as a guide.

1. Choose a short paragraph or section.

2. Read the passage at least ten times.

3. Use a dictionary to look up unfamiliar words.

4. Notice any repetitive words or ideas.

5. List the main characters and their roles in the incident.

6. Try to determine why the Lord included this passage in the Bible.

7. Decide upon the main subject of the passage and express it in one or two words. Examples include sin, faith, repentance, God's love, etc.

8. Write a simple sentence on what the passage teaches about the subject. Example: Man must repent in order to enter the kingdom.

9. Determine whether the sentence accurately reflects the intent of the text by rereading the passage several times.

10. Revise the sentence as needed.

---

spoke of God the Father's plan regarding the role of the religious leaders in Christ's death. Peter probably recalled Jesus' teaching when he preached on the day of Pentecost in Acts 2. "Him, being delivered by the determinate counsel and foreknowledge of God, ye have taken, and by wicked hands have crucified and slain" (Acts 2:23). Notice too that Jesus twice used the word *kill* to describe what would happen in Jerusalem. Again, the disciples failed to understand and were afraid to ask (Mark 9:32).

Later, Jesus led the disciples to Jerusalem (Mark 10:32-34). Their fear and amazement indicates that they knew what was likely to happen. Perhaps they believed His words, but simply could not comprehend all that He said. The fact that Jesus again explicitly told them what would happen points to His knowledge as God. He both knew the situation and controlled the situation. This created real fear in the disciples, but later, it would be a great comfort. The death of their Master was not an accident. He planned to die for them. Notice that Jesus used eight verbs to describe the events in Jerusalem. The final one should give them hope during the trials that lay ahead. Jesus would rise from the dead. They simply needed to believe and to trust in all that Jesus said.

Dangers for the Disciples
Mark 9:33-50

Immediately following the second of Jesus' teachings about His death, the disciples argued about which one of them would be the greatest in the kingdom. They thought that Jesus did not know about the conflict and seemed to be embarrassed when He asked them about it (Mark 9:34). Christ took this problem as an opening to discuss many dangers that the disciples currently faced and would face to an even greater extent in the future. But, in order to understand Jesus' intention, we need to examine His conclusion before we look at each potential problem.

One well-respected Bible scholar believes that Mark 9:49 and 50 are the two hardest verses in the New Testament to interpret (Hiebert, 269). Our western thought patterns are not like those in the ancient Near East. The best we can do is capture the essence of the meaning; some of the details and logic will elude us. The verses start with the word *for,* which tells us that Jesus is drawing a conclusion to the entire section. Salt was commonly used in Palestine as a preservative. Its necessity for life made salt a valuable commodity. Some ancient cultures used it in treaties as a symbol of good intentions or genuineness. The disciples would also recognize it as a necessary part of Old Testament sacrifices. Salt therefore seems to point to the purification and veracity of a relationship.

Jesus makes a connection between salt and fire in verse 49. John the Baptist preached that Jesus would baptize people with the Holy Spirit and fire (Matt. 3:11). An Old Testament believer would see salt as a symbol of a relationship with God. The New Testament believer would see fire in the same manner. In verse 50, Jesus says that the believer's effectiveness can be lost just as salt can lose its taste. Jesus implies that wrongful dealings with others can spoil our effectiveness in the kingdom. The power and purifying aspects of our relationship to God must spill over to our dealings with other believers. Jesus gives us three interconnected categories of danger that can ruin our service to God and our relationships to others.

First, personal ambition has no place in God's kingdom (Mark 9:34-37). Jesus answered the disciples' question about who should be greatest by exalting service. The greatest would be the servant. Jesus served God, and He also served the disciples in numerous ways. They should do the same. Notice too that the object of the service must include those who are weakest and most vulnerable in the kingdom. Jesus saw the child's innocent faith. The disciples must receive children. Instead of exalting self, a true disciple will serve those who respond to Christ.

Second, petty divisions among believers have no place in God's kingdom (Mark 9:38-41). The disciples stopped a man who was casting out unclean spirits in Jesus' name. Christ's words and actions made deep divisions among the Jews. Those who hated Jesus would logically not do anything to further His cause. The others, however, responded to Christ—as evidenced by their actions. The disciples must not do anything to extinguish the active faith of others. God commended the efforts of those who would do something as small as giving a cup of water. They must likewise commend the efforts of others who work for Christ.

Third, actions that lead to sin have no place in God's kingdom (Mark 9:42-48). The Greek word *offend* means much more than doing something that annoys or embarrasses. It means "to stumble" or "to cause to sin." Notice that Jesus first applies the principle to children or, by interpretation, those who respond but are weak. The disciple must ever be careful to nurture and not destroy the faith of others. Jesus also applies it to personal issues. Cutting off the hand or foot is a figure of speech. Anything that might hinder our entrance into the kingdom must be terminated. The disciple must therefore guard his own faith to ensure a positive response to Christ.

Lessons with the King
Mark 11:1-26

Jesus now approached the city of Jerusalem. The time was short, and the disciples still required much training. They needed to concentrate on Christ's deity and on His expectation for them. The twelve would then be ready to face His humiliation and death. Jesus taught them a lesson in basic discipleship. He commanded two of them to go into a nearby village to obtain a colt. He also told them how to answer anyone who asked why they were taking the colt. As God, He knew the animal's location and that the owners would release it to the disciples. They found the animal just as Jesus said. Christ's words were completely trustworthy. Obedience led to a better appreciation of His greatness.

Jesus rode the donkey toward the city. The Old Testament prophets had spoken of Messiah's entry into the city on a donkey (Zech. 9:9). People visiting Jerusalem for the Passover celebration now came out to welcome Jesus. They spread clothing and tree branches in the road as He passed by. Others joined in a procession to the city. All cried out, "Hosanna: Blessed is he that cometh in the name of the Lord." The disciples would know that the cry was a quote from Psalm 118 about the Messiah. Jesus did not restrain the crowds. He publicly presented Himself as their Messiah and King.

Jesus spent the night outside Jerusalem in the small village of Bethany. The visiting crowds praised Jesus as Messiah, but the religious leadership viewed Him differently. Bethany offered a safe haven for rest. The next day He returned to the temple to display His authority as King. You will remember that the priests sold animals for sacrifice and exchanged foreign coins within and around the temple. Their corrupt practices were well known in the ancient world. Jesus overturned the tables of money and expelled the merchants. He further quoted from the prophets to explain His actions to the multitude. The priests had turned the temple into a robber's den. God intended it to be a place where He could meet His people. Jesus the Messiah was simply restoring God's original purpose for this holy place. The disciples saw Jesus' zeal to do the will of God and to judge wicked religion. Only fear of the crowds prevented the scribes and priests from immediately destroying Jesus.

The Lord had one other private lesson for the disciples (Mark 11:12-14, 20-26). Jesus was hungry and saw a fig tree near the road. Upon examination, He found no figs on the tree, and so He said that no one would ever eat from the tree again. Christ judged the tree for a lack of fruit. Many theologians see a parallel to Christ's judgment on the nation of Israel for lack of response to His teaching. The next day as they walked along the same path, Peter saw that the tree was withered from the roots upward. Peter's amazement shows his lack of faith in Christ's words. This time, Jesus moved to the very heart of Peter's problem by encouraging him to "Have faith in God" (Mark 11:22). Mountain moving was a common figure of speech. The Jews used it to refer to God's power. Jesus told them that anything was possible for those who believe God and who forgive their fellow man.

Communion with Christ
Mark 14:12-25

Personal fellowship with Christ is perhaps the most important aspect of discipleship. Without it, our spiritual lives dry up, leaving the shell of dead religion. Jesus actively sought for this time of communion. The Passover meal was a high point in the Jewish religious year. Eating this special meal together was a symbol of His close relationship with the disciples. His instructions to two of the disciples about where to prepare the Passover are similar to His words regarding finding the donkey. Jesus described a specific set of circumstances. Women generally carried water. Therefore, the two disciples could easily identify the right man since he would have a pitcher of water. Mark records that they "found as he had said unto them" (Mark 14:16), which indicates that the disciples believed that Jesus' words were more than mere coincidence. As deity, He directed them to the appointed place and gave them the job of preparing the meal. As disciples, they obeyed the Master's direction and worked accordingly.

The actual preparation probably took most of the day. They followed the Jewish ritual of removing any trace of leaven from the house, and they also procured the food. At evening, Jesus and the disciples came to the house and started the ceremonial meal. Jesus told the twelve that one of them was a traitor. One by one they asked Him, "Is it I?" The grammatical form indicates that the asker expected a negative response. Almost every follower of Christ passes through periods of doubt, which are indications of a tender heart. Jesus knew Judas Iscariot's intentions. Mark 14:21 may have been Christ's final offer of mercy to Judas. Most Bible scholars believe that at this time Judas departed from the room.

Jesus then instituted what we know as the Lord's Supper or communion (Mark 14:22-26). His words placed new significance on the bread and wine, which were parts of the traditional Passover observance. The bread symbolized Christ's body. He explained the wine as "my blood of the new testament, which is shed for many." In the Old Testament, Moses sealed the relationship between God and the people by sprinkling blood upon them (Exod. 24:8 ff.). God granted cleansing from sin through the blood of a sacrifice (Lev. 17:11). Additionally, through the prophet Jeremiah, God had promised that a new covenant would eventually replace the old one. Believers would have God's Word in their hearts, and they would enjoy close fellowship with Him (Jer. 31:31-34). Jesus taught the disciples that His death would establish the new covenant. His blood sealed their relationship with God. By consuming the symbolic bread and wine, the disciples showed their agreement with God's purposes for Christ's ministry and death. Christ commanded the disciples to regularly observe this simple meal as a remembrance of Him (Luke 22:19). Followers of Christ find their greatest joy and strength in remembering the Savior.

The School of Failure

Military leaders know from history and from experience that battles bring to light the integrity of an army. Christ's trial and crucifixion would severely test the disciples' character. Their utter failures would give Christ the opportunity to show them His gracious compassion. The disciples would never be the same.

Following the Lord's Supper, Jesus led the band to the Mount of Olives. He announced that all eleven would depart from Him that very evening. He quoted from Zechariah 13:7 to reinforce the reality of their weakness. Peter and the others affirmed that they would never leave. Remember that all asked, "Is it I?" when Jesus told them about the traitor. Now they refused to hear Christ's words and the Old Testament Scriptures. Jesus told Peter that he would deny Him three times before the rooster crowed twice in the morning. Again, Peter hardened himself and vehemently refused to believe His Master's warning.

Next, Jesus went to the garden of Gethsemane to pray for grace and strength. He separated Peter, James, and John from the others to accompany Him to a secluded place. His struggles at this point would be private, except for the three who were to act as guards. As Jesus prayed, they went to sleep. He woke them up and returned to prayer only to find them asleep again. Jesus woke them up a second and a third time. "Couldest not thou watch one hour?" (Mark 14:37) was a stiff rebuke for someone who had just affirmed his loyalty unto death. Peter could not even discipline his body's need for sleep for an hour of prayer.

Learning from Christ Today

The disciples often listened to Jesus Christ as they walked from one place to another. He actively sought times to teach them away from the noisy crowds. Jesus wants the same opportunity with us. Living for Christ means learning how to fellowship with Him daily through personal devotions. Use the following suggestions to guide your communication with the Savior.

1. Read the Bible: Ask God to teach you something that you need that day, and then systematically read through the Bible. Bible reading schedules are available from the Internet or your church. Write down in a notebook the specific things that God impresses upon your mind. Tell someone about what you found.

2. Meditate on the Bible: Meditation simply means to regularly think about something. It is a deliberate act of the mind. An easy way to meditate is to mark verses in your Bible that God shows you in your reading and then memorize them. Look for specific applications to your life and obey God regarding the principle.

3. Pray every day: In a journal, write down your requests to God and His answers. His faithfulness will greatly encourage you. Keep a balance between requests and praise by using the ACT formula. *A* stands for adoring God for His person and greatness. *C* stands for confessing your sins and failures. *T* stands for thanking Him for what He has done and will do.

(Based on *Basics for Believers,* James A. Berg, BJUP, 1978, pp. 18, 19.)

Judas and a band from the religious leaders then entered the garden and approached Jesus. Judas identified Jesus with a kiss of greeting. The mob then arrested Christ. Peter took a sword and cut off the ear of one of the servants (Mark 14:47; John 18:10). We can only speculate about Peter's motivation. What could one person do against a mob? How did he manage to cut off the servant's ear? Did he raise the sword over the man's head and wildly swing it down toward his body? A trained soldier would use horizontal thrusts to disable an enemy. Foolish zeal seems to have seized the disobedient Peter.

The mob led Jesus away to an illegal trial before the Sanhedrin. Peter followed far behind and tried to blend into the crowd of servants near the inquiry (Mark 14:54). He evidently wanted to see what would happen. On two occasions a small girl identified Peter as a follower of Christ. Peter denied it both times. Finally one of the servants accused Peter of being a follower of Christ, and this time he supplemented his denial with cursing and swearing. When the rooster crowed for a second time, Peter remembered the words of Christ. Peter cried bitterly over his failures (Mark 14:72).

PRINCIPLES

APPLIED

Peter's Epistles

The Gospel of John gives an extended account of Christ's dealing with and restoring Peter after the resurrection. Peter went on to preach mighty sermons, to witness to the Jewish nation, and to write two letters about his faith in Christ. The letters show us that Christ's life and work forever shaped and molded Peter's thoughts. Look up the following verses in Peter's Epistles, determine the event referred to, and then find the corresponding section in Mark. Remember that a true disciple of Christ will know and concentrate upon the words and deeds of his Master.

I Peter 1:3 _____

I Peter 1:11 _____

_____

I Peter 1:18, 19 _____

_____

I Peter 2:6-8 _____

I Peter 2:22-25 _____

_____

II Peter 1:16-21 _____

The high priest and Sanhedrin delivered Jesus to Pontius Pilate for crucifixion. For six hours the Messiah hung on a cross in sheer agony. He died as the Jews mocked Him. Mark does not tell us the location of the eleven disciples during this time. They probably hid themselves, fearing that they too would be crucified. Did they agonize over the loss of their master? Did they cry over their own failures? Did they mourn the loss of a high position in the kingdom? All are likely true.

Jesus had told the disciples repeatedly that He would rise from the dead on the third day following His death. Two women went to the tomb to prepare His body for burial, and an angel greeted them. He announced Christ's Resurrection! The women were to go and "tell his disciples and **Peter** that he goeth before you to Galilee: there shall ye see him, as he said unto you [emphasis added]" (Mark 16:7). Jesus appeared to at least three other individuals who told the news to the disciples. The eleven did not believe that Jesus was alive. Finally, Jesus appeared to them and strongly rebuked their unresponsive hearts (Mark 16:14). He told them to go into the entire world and tell people about His great salvation for man's sins. Notice that even though the disciples miserably failed Jesus at the trial and crucifixion, He sought them and forgave them. Over the next years, the disciples preached to the entire known world, and scores were saved. The disciples' actions proved the reality of Christ's compassion in their own lives. The rest of their lives would now be spent telling others about Jesus Christ's love for sinners.

Knowing Christ

The Gospel of Mark starts by proclaiming that Jesus Christ is the Son of God. His deity forms the backbone of the book. We have examined Christ's relationship to various groups of people. As both God and man, Jesus healed the sick, cast out unclean spirits, calmed the sea, rebuked religious leaders, trained His disciples, and died for sinners. Through these events, the Lord wants us to know and to understand His Son. The crucifixion of Christ forced the disciples to see themselves as weak and sinful. His Resurrection and compassion forced the disciples to transfer the facts about Christ from their heads into their hearts. Christianity is not a philosophy or a religion. It is a relationship between a believer and the Son of God. That relationship transformed Peter's cowardly denials of his Lord into bold proclamations of God's grace both in Jerusalem and around the Roman world. Peter and the disciples saw Jesus Christ in person. Mark wrote his Gospel for our benefit that we too might see Jesus. The key to a full life in this world and to eternal life in heaven is "that I may know him."

Review Questions

1. What Old Testament men appeared with Christ at the transfiguration?

2. Whose ministry did Jesus equate with John the Baptist's?

3. Who betrayed Jesus to the mob?

4. Who would be the greatest in the kingdom according to Jesus?

5. The word *offend* means what?

6. How did Jesus arrive in Jerusalem?

7. What did Jesus curse as a lesson on faith for the disciples?

8. The Lord's Supper is closely associated with what Jewish observance?

9. Where was Jesus betrayed?

10. Who told the two women about Christ's resurrection?

Essay

Write one or two complete sentences to answer the following questions.

11. Why was Jesus transfigured?

12. How do we know that Jesus' death was not an accident?

13. What is the symbolic significance of salt in Mark 9?

14. What is the significance of the bread and wine at the Lord's Supper?

15. Why did Peter weep when the rooster crowed the second time?

Photograph Credits

The following agencies and individuals have furnished materials to meet the photographic needs of this textbook. We wish to express our gratitude to them for their important contribution.

1999-2001 www.arttoday.com
American Tract Society www.ATStracts.org
Bob Jones University Collection
Christian History Institute
Mike James
Overseas Missionary Fellowship

Chapter 1
Mike James 4; *Mark* by Guido Reni, The Bob Jones University Collection 5

Chapter 2
1999-2001 www.arttoday.com 21; Mike James 26; Overseas Missionary Fellowship 31

Chapter 3
Christian History Institute 50

Chapter 5
The BJU Press Files 88; *The Mocking of Christ* by Northern follower of Caravaggio, The Bob Jones University Collection 92

Chapter 6
American Tract Society, www.ATStracts.org 102

Chapter 7
The Christ of Derision by Philippe de Champaigne, The Bob Jones University Collection 116